CAN MAZER STUMP YOU?

1 Which team had the best season in baseball history and when?

2 Who hit the first modern World Series home run?

3 What did Joe DiMaggio, Ted Williams, Joe Gordon, Chuck Klein, Mel Ott, and Babe Ruth have in common?

4 Which team holds the record for most runs scored in one inning?

5 Who is the only man to have played in both the Little League World Series and a major league World Series?

6 Which team had the worst losing streak in baseball?

7 Which noted pitcher became Henry Aaron's most frequent home run victim?

8 When and where was the first National League game played?

9 Who was the king of runs-batted-in before Hack Wilson hit 190 in one season?

10 Who was the "clown prince" of baseball?

For extra credit: Who hit the line drive into Dizzy Dean's big toe?

(answers on page 2)

Answers:

1 The 1906 Chicago Cubs won 116 and lost only 36 for a winning percentage of .763.
2 Jim Sebring of the Pittsburgh Pirates.
3 Each player hit as many or more home runs in a single season as an entire team did during that season.
4 In 1953 the Boston Red Sox scored 17 runs in the seventh inning against the Detroit Tigers.
5 Boog Powell
6 The Philadelphia Phillies of 1961 lost 23 in a row in August.
7 Don Drysdale
8 Philadelphia on Saturday, April 22, 1876. The teams were the Athletics and the Boston Red Stockings.
9 Lou Gehrig
10 Al Schacht of the Washington Senators
Extra credit: Earl Averill

THE AMAZIN' BILL MAZER'S BASEBALL TRIVIA BOOK

WARNER BOOKS

A Warner Communications Company

To all the trivia buffs of the world.

ACKNOWLEDGEMENTS

The authors wish to thank the following people, without whom this book could not have been written: Dave Lippman, who was of extraordinary assistance on research and qualifies for an "Amazin' Mazer" bumper sticker, at the very least; and Lori Weisman, for her patience, fortitude, and encouragement in typing the manuscript. Not to mention Andrew Lippman, Richard Friedman, Michael Fleming, George Hall, Stewart Scharf, David Borsack, Matt Scheckner, Mike Barnes, Jory Levinton, Gabe Miller, Joe Carbone, Errol Somay, Jim Namrow, Nate Salant, Matthew Ryan and Chris Pellettieri, each of whom contributed ideas and assistance in one way or another.

Finally, a tip of the hat is in order for our editor, John Kinney, who encouraged us on this project; not to mention the splendid work of our copy editor, and Chicago White Sox loyalist, Dan Flanagan.

THE AMAZIN'
BILL MAZER'S
BASEBALL
TRIVIA
BOOK

THIS CANADIAN-BORN SLUGGER ALMOST WON A BATTING TITLE WITH THE BROOKLYN DODGERS. DO YOU KNOW WHO HE IS?

Goodwin George (Goody) Rosen of Toronto.

In 1945, Rosen batted .325. "I should have won the battin' championship that year, the way I was hittin' into September," said Rosen. "Tommy Holmes [Boston Braves] and I were neck-and-neck most of the season. But I'm playin' center field between Dixie Walker and Augie Galan. Neither of them had any speed—they wore me out.

"We go into Philadelphia—worst team in the league. Seven games. That's where I should have picked up some ground. Instead of that, I only get five hits in thirty-three times at bat. Naw, it wasn't their pitching. I was makin' contact. Just kept hittin' the ball right at somebody."

Goody got his lumps in his second season in the majors, crashing into a wall in St. Louis. "Honest," he insists, "with the ability I had there's no telling how good I might have been if I hadn't run into the wall.

"I used to fight with our manager in Brooklyn, Leo Durocher, all the time. One year, I guess it was 1939, I'd been leadin' the league for the first month-and-a-half. Now I tear up an ankle. Durocher comes to me crying that I'm the team leader and he needs me in there every day. So I continue to play on that bum ankle. My battin' average does a dive and I wind up gettin' sent down to Montreal."

Goody recalls Branch Rickey, the man who traded him from the Dodgers to the Giants. "In a way, he did give notice that I'd be going," Rosen admits. "During the winter, he had asked me to come down and discuss contracts. I told him what I wanted. He said he'd pay it but that he'd have to trade me.

"But I start the season with the club and everything seems to be okay. Now we have a series with the Giants at the Polo Grounds. I'm on my way to the ball park on the subway. I pick up a copy of the old *New York Mirror*. There's the headline: 'ROSEN SOLD TO THE GIANTS FOR $50,000 AND TWO PLAYERS.' That's how I find out I've been traded.

"We played a doubleheader that day, and if I say it myself, they couldn't get me out. By the time the two games were over, I had muscle spasms in my legs. You should have heard that Durocher givin' it to me."

BROOKLYN DODGERS' MANAGER WILBERT "UNCLE ROBBIE" ROBINSON ONCE GAVE A FAN A FREE SEASON'S PASS TO ALL OF THE DODGERS HOME GAMES AT EBBETS FIELD. A WEEK LATER THE FAN GAVE THE PASS BACK. WHY?

A regular rooter known locally as Abie the Iceman would take his afternoons off and visit Ebbets Field. Once there he would jeer the Dodgers. "Ya bums, ya," he'd shout in a raspy voice. His yelling annoyed some of the Dodgers, so one day, Robinson asked Abie if he would like to get into games free, and offered him a season's pass. There was one condition—Abie had to stop yelling at Robinson's players.

The Iceman liked the deal and accepted. Just one week later Abie returned the pass to Robinson. "I can't take it anymore," he explained. "Here's your pass. I gotta yell—'cause they ARE bums."

WHO MADE THE MOST PITCHING APPEARANCES IN A WORLD SERIES?

Darold Knowles of the Oakland Athletics emerged from the bullpen seven times in the 1973 World Series.

In those seven games, he compiled a 0.00 earned-run average (ERA) in 6⅓ innings. Knowles did not win or lose any of the games, but he did tie the record for most games saved in a World Series, with two.

Originally, Knowles came up with the Washington Senators, with whom in four consecutive years he produced an ERA of under 3.00. In one of those years, 1970, he lost 14 games, tying the record for relief pitchers. (That was more a tribute to the old Senators' pitiful offense and defense.) He was traded to Oakland in the middle of 1971 for Don Mincher, Paul Lindblad, and Mike Epstein, and with the Athletics' famed Mustache Gang, he came up with a 1.36 ERA in 1972 as a reliever.

At the end of 1974, the A's traded Knowles, Bob Locker, and Manny Trillo to the Chicago Cubs for Billy Williams. With the Cubs, he posted a 5.83 ERA in 1975, and then a 2.88 ERA in 1976. From there he went to the Texas Rangers, and thence to the Expos, where he had a 2.38 ERA. In 1980 he pitched for the St. Louis Cardinals.

Although Knowles was an effective reliever, he was rarely a .500 pitcher, even with the A's. Nevertheless, in 1973 he put on a marvelous and memorable display of relief pitching.

WHO WAS THE FIRST MAN IN THE MODERN ERA OF BASEBALL TO LEAD THE NATIONAL LEAGUE IN THE EARNED-RUN AVERAGE DEPARTMENT?

In his first year (1912), Charles Monroe "Jeff" Tesreau, led the National League with a brilliant 1.96 ERA. A 6'2" spitballer, he went 17–7 for the New York Giants. Tesreau was a member of one of the finest pitching staffs in history; along with Tesreau, it comprised Christy Mathewson, Rube Marquard, Red Ames, Doc Crandall and George "Hooks" Wiltse.

Tesreau had a 22–13 won–lost record in 1913, and then went 26–10 in 1914. But he faded to 14–14 the next year, 13–8 the year after that, and quit baseball in 1918 after an abysmal 4–4 season.

Big Jeff was lucky enough to have had a sparkling ERA in the year that earned-run average was introduced as a statistic in the National League. The first official ERAs for the American League were recorded in 1913, when Walter Johnson of the Washington Senators led with a 1.09 mark.

The Giant rookie's mark only lasted two years, when Spittin' Bill Doak posted a 1.72 mark for the St. Louis Cardinals while working his way to a 19–6 season. Both Tesreau and Doak relied on the now-illegal spitball.

WHO WAS THE KING OF RUNS BATTED IN BEFORE HACK WILSON HIT 190 IN ONE SEASON?

Lou Gehrig.

While the great Babe Ruth hammered out 60 home runs in 1927, his cohort Lou Gehrig was clouting 54 home runs, with 175 runs batted in (RBIs) and a .373 average.

The key to Gehrig's success was that he hit fourth in the New York Yankees' batting order, right behind The Babe. Thus, Gehrig had a better chance of coming up with men on base than Ruth did. Ruth hit .356 that year, so that when he didn't hit a four-bagger he often got on base another way. Lou would then hit a homer or a double, enabling Ruth and often other teammates to score.

The slugging of Ruth and Gehrig helped the 1927 Yankees to a pennant and to a four-game sweep over the Pittsburgh Pirates in the World Series.

Hack Wilson's 190 RBIs helped spearhead the Chicago Cubs during the 1930 pennant race, but the

Cubs finished two games behind the St. Louis Cardinals.

NAME THE ONLY PLAYER IN BASEBALL WHOSE LAST NAME CONTAINS ALL FIVE VOWELS OF THE ALPHABET.

Not only was Ed Figueroa the first Puerto Rican 20-game winner, but he has all five vowels in his last name, and each vowel appears only once.

Figgy made his debut with the California Angels in 1974. In his first full season (1975) he was 16–13 with a 2.90 ERA. The 6'1" pitcher was traded to the Yankees with Mickey Rivers for Bobby Bonds in 1976.

In 1976 he was 19–10, with a 3.01 ERA; in 1977 he was 16–11, with a 3.58 ERA; and in 1978 he achieved the 20-win milestone with a 20–9 season, going the distance on the next-to-last day of the season to win number 20. Another Figueroa, José (no relation to Ed) played outfield for the Chicago Cubs in 1980.

Two players in the majors have first names containing all five vowels: Aurelio Rodriguez of the Tigers, Padres and Aurelio Lopez of the St. Louis Cardinals. But nobody before has had all five vowels in his last name.

WHAT PITCHER WON THE MOST GAMES IN A SEASON WITHOUT A DEFEAT?

Tom Zachary, who is best known for giving up number 60 to Babe Ruth in 1927, pitched 26 games for the New York Yankees in 1929, winning 12 and

16

losing none. That 1929 campaign was one of Zachary's rare winning seasons—he was a lifetime 186–191 pitcher.

A Washington Senators' mainstay for many years, Zachary came to the Yankees in 1928, following his climactic final game of the previous season, in which Ruth hit his immortal number 60. He spent most of his time with the Yankees as a spot starter and only got his 26 starts in 1929 because the Yankees were wracked with injuries. Zachary was 12–15 in 1924, when the Senators won the pennant, and 14–15 the following year, when the Senators repeated on top.

In 1912, Rube Marquard won 19 for the New York Giants before losing a game, and Ron Guidry in 1978 won 15 before suffering his first loss with the Yankees.

CAN YOU RECALL SOME OF THE RECORDS SET BY THE ORIGINAL METS?

Pitcher Roger Craig lost the most games (25) in a single season in National League's history. The Mets lost the most games (120) and finished with an all-time low .250 winning percentage.

On the plus side, the Mets set a record for highest attendance for a last-place club, and Gil Hodges established himself as all-time king of home-run-hitting first basemen, reaching a lifetime total of 370.

The Mets' most unusual mark was that they were the first team in major league history to have two players with exactly the same name—pitchers Robert L. "Lefty" Miller and Robert G. "Righty" Miller. Both were original Mets. Robert L. Miller won one and lost 12, compiling a 4.88 ERA. He came back to the Mets in 1974 to win two and lose two, in his final year in the big leagues. Robert G. Miller had an equally uninspiring record, winning two and losing two for the 1962 Mets.

No other team in history has had two players with the same name. (By the way, the Millers were not related.)

NAME THE ONLY PLAYERS OF THE 1980s WHO WEAR NUMBERS 0 AND 00 (DOUBLE ZERO)?

Al Oliver, the veteran Texas Rangers' outfielder, asked for and got number 0 when he was traded to Texas. The zero is actually an O, for Oliver.

The man with the double zero was Bobby Bonds, who in 1980 played for the St. Louis Cardinals. Bonds, who has hit 30 home runs and stolen 30 bases on five different occasions in the majors, hit a grand slam in his first major league game and has well over 300 career home runs. He also has led each league in striking out several times and has been on seven different teams: the Giants, the Yankees, the Angels, the Rangers, the Indians, the White Sox, and the Cardinals.

In recent baseball history there have been others who wore a zero, George Scott of the Kansas City Royals among them. But only Bonds and Oliver wore the zero in 1980.

ONLY ONE TIME IN MAJOR LEAGUE BASEBALL HISTORY DID THREE TEAMS OPPOSE EACH OTHER IN THE SAME GAME. WHAT WHERE THE CIRCUMSTANCES LEADING TO THIS BIZARRE DEVELOPMENT?

It happened June 26, 1944, at the Polo Grounds in New York. The teams involved were the Brooklyn Dodgers, New York Yankees, and New York Giants. The game was staged as a gimmick to raise money for United States war bonds during World War II.

Each team played successive innings against the other two and then sat out for an inning. The six-inning exhibition proved a huge success, drawing more than 50,000 fans.

The Dodgers hold the distinction of beating two teams in one game, 5–1–0.

The linescore for the game:

Brooklyn Dodgers: 120 002—5
New York Yankees: 000 001—1
New York Giants: 000 000—0

WHAT TEAM HOLDS THE RECORD FOR MOST RUNS SCORED IN ONE INNING?

The Brooklyn Dodgers scored a whopping 15 runs in the first inning of a game against the Cincinnati Reds on May 21, 1952. The outburst set numerous records that still stand today, including most runs in one inning (15), most runs scored in the first inning (15), most runs scored with two outs (12), most players to come to bat in one inning (21) and most batters to reach base safely in succession (19).

The inning evolved as follows: Billy Cox grounded out; Pee Wee Reese walked; Duke Snider homered to right (2–0); Jackie Robinson doubled to left; Andy Pafko walked; George Shuba singled Robinson home and Pafko to second; after Reds pitcher Ewell Blackwell was replaced by Bud Byerly, Pafko was thrown out trying to steal third, as Shuba went to second; Gil Hodges walked; Rube Walker singled Shuba home; Chris Van Cuyk singled home Hodges; Cox singled home Walker; Reese singled home Van Cuyk to make it 7–0; Byerly was replaced by Herm Wehmeier; Snider walked to load the bases; Robinson was hit by a pitch, Cox scoring on the play; Pafko singled home Reese and Snider; Frank Smith relieved Wehmeier with the score 10–0; Shuba walked to load the bases; Hodges walked to force in Robinson; Walker singled home Pafko and Shuba; Van Cuyk singled in Hodges for the 14th run; Cox was hit by a pitch to load the bases; Reese walked to force in Walker; Snider struck out. Totals: 15 runs, 10 hits, seven walks, two batters hit by a pitch; three men left on base.

WHO IS THE ONLY MAJOR LEAGUE PLAYER TO HIT A FAIR BALL OUT OF DODGER STADIUM? (HINT: HE DID IT TWICE.)

Willie Stargell, the Most Valuable Player in the 1979 World Series, is the man who accomplished the feat.

His first blow came off Alan Foster on August 6, 1969. The roundtripper cleared the right-field pavilion and was measured at 506 feet and six inches.

Stargell's second clout was off hurler Andy Messersmith on May 8, 1973. The ball also cleared the right-field pavilion and was measured at 470 feet.

One of the most thrilling moments in baseball developed during the 1978 American League playoff game between the Boston Red Sox and the New York Yankees, held on October 2, 1978, at Fenway Park. The Yankees won the game, but only after a series of heroic events. Let's see how much you remember.

WHEN BUCKY DENT HIT HIS THREE-RUN HOMER FOR THE YANKEES IN THE SEVENTH INNING, WHO WAS ON BASE?

Roy White and Chris Chambliss, both of whom had singled.

HOW MANY WERE OUT WHEN DENT HIT THE HOME RUN?

There were two out. Graig Nettles had opened the inning by flying out to right. Then Chambliss and White singled and Jim Spencer pinch-hit for Brian Doyle and flied out to left.

WHAT WAS THE COUNT ON DENT BEFORE HE HIT THE HOME RUN?

Bucky took the first pitch for a ball and fouled the second pitch off his foot. The count was 1–1 when he walloped a pitch just over the left-field wall.

DENT WAS BATTING BECAUSE . . .

In 1977 Bucky nearly quit the Yankees because he was constantly being taken out of the lineup by manager Billy Martin for a pinch hitter. After Bob Lemon replaced Martin, Dent batted more often. Nevertheless, Bucky still should have been removed in that particular situation. There were two out, the Red Sox' Mike Torrez was a right-handed pitcher who was throwing well, and Dent was a right-handed batter who had not impressed Torrez on that day. Under normal circumstances Dent would have been yanked. But these were not normal circumstances because the Yankees were dreadfully short of infielders. Second baseman Willie Randolph had pulled a hamstring muscle in a game against Cleveland three days earlier. Brian Doyle started the game at second but Spencer had pinch-hit for him. That meant that the Yankees' only remaining healthy infielder, Fred Stanley, would be moved to second base. The only alternative was to pinch-hit for Dent and then have Stanley play short-stop, and outfielder Paul Blair play second.

APART FROM BUCKY DENT AND MIKE TORREZ, ONE OTHER PLAYER FIGURED PROMINENTLY IN DENT'S HOME RUN. WHO WAS HE?

Mickey Rivers.

After Dent had fouled Torrez's second pitch off his foot, Bucky was handed a bat that belonged to Rivers. Mickey had told the batboy to give the bat to Dent and "tell him to hit a home run with it." Seconds after the home run had been hit, Dent crossed the plate to the cheers of his teammates. Rivers was there, of course, laughing and shouting at Dent. It's almost as if Mickey knew what would happen all the time.

IN 1961 ROGER MARIS OF THE NEW YORK YANKEES HIT A RECORD-BREAKING 61 HOME RUNS. HOW MANY TIMES WAS HE INTENTIONALLY WALKED THAT SEASON?

None. As it happened, Maris batted immediately before Mickey Mantle in the lineup. Despite Roger's awesome slugging ability, few pitchers cared to walk him in order to pitch to Mantle, who hit .317 that year, along with 54 homers and 128 runs batted in. Mantle received a total of nine intentional walks in 1961.

THE SAME PITCHER WHO GAVE UP
ROGER MARIS'S 60th HOME RUN ALSO GAVE
UP TED WILLIAM'S 521st AND LAST HOME
RUN, IN WILLIAM'S FINAL AT BAT. WHO WAS
THAT PITCHER?

Jack Fisher.

TY COBB IS THE MAJOR LEAGUE LEADER
IN LIFETIME BATTING AVERAGE (.367), BAT-
TING TITLES WON (12), AND BASE HITS
(4,191). COBB ALSO WAS ONE OF THE MOST
AGGRESSIVE PLAYERS IN HISTORY, BOTH ON
AND OFF THE FIELD. THERE IS A POPULAR
THEORY AS TO PRECISELY WHY COBB WAS
SO AGGRESSIVE. CAN YOU EXPLAIN WHY?

According to the respected author Al Stump, who
helped Cobb write his autobiography during the last
months of Ty's life, Cobb was haunted by a feeling
that his dead father was always watching him. Cobb's
father was a state senator and a scholar, and Ty idol-
ized him. On an August night in 1905, Ty's father told
his family that he was going by buggy, to a nearby
town. But, suspecting that his wife had been un-
faithful to him, he doubled back and climbed into
his wife's bedroom through the window. Hearing
strange noises, Mrs. Cobb assumed a burglar was on
the premises. She grabbed a shotgun and killed the
intruder, who happened to be her husband. Stump
and others believe that this tragic event shaped Cobb's
personality. In *Ty Cobb's Wild Ten Month Fight to
Live*, Stump writes that from the moment Ty learned
of his father's death, he became "a vindicator who
believed that 'Father was watching' and could not

put his father's terrible fate out of his mind. The memory of it threatened his sanity." Stump believes that "the violent death of a father whom a sensitive, highly-talented boy loved deeply and feared, engendered, through some strangely supreme desire to vindicate that father, the most violent, successful, thoroughly maladjusted personality ever to pass across American sports. The shock tipped the 18-year-old mind, making him capable of incredible feats. . . ."

Others recognized that there was a very special fire burning within Cobb. Casey Stengel once said. "I never saw anyone like Cobb. No one even close to him. When he wiggled those wild eyes at a pitcher you knew you were looking at the one bird nobody could beat. It was like he was superhuman."

Cobb, who fought and scuffled with players on the field and with bartenders, croupiers in casinos, and just about anyone else who would fight him off the field, told author Al Stump his own theory of what prompted his unusually aggressive behavior. "I was like a steel spring with a growing and dangerous flaw in it. If it is wound too tight or has the slighest weak point, the spring will fly apart and then it is done for. . . ."

OUR NATIONAL ANTHEM, "THE-STAR SPANGLED BANNER," ONCE WAS BOOED WHEN IT WAS PLAYED AT A WORLD SERIES GAME. DO YOU REMEMBER WHERE AND WHY?

Prior to game five of the 1968 classic, held on October 7 at Briggs Stadium in Detroit, the 23-year-old blind Puerto Rican singer José Feliciano delivered the anthem with a blend of soul and folksinging. The unique performance angered many of the fans at the Tigers-Cardinals contest and inspired protests from many who were watching on television. *The New York Times* reported that Feliciano was booed "by many in the crowd of 53,634." Tiger's shortstop Ray Oyler's brother Joe described Feliciano's version of the anthem as "unpatriotic." A fan, Mrs. Arlene Raicevich, said she was so upset that she planned to write her senator about it. The National Broadcasting Company, which televised the game, revealed that its New York office received 400 protest phone calls.

SIX AMERICAN-BORN BLACK PITCHERS HAVE WON WORLD SERIES GAMES. CAN YOU NAME THEM?

Bob Gibson is the best-known of the Negro hurlers; he won seven games in nine decisions with the St. Louis Cardinals in 1964, 1967, and 1968. The others are Joe Black, with the Brooklyn Dodgers in 1952; Jim "Mudcat" Grant, with the Minnesota Twins in 1965; John Wyatt, with the Boston Red Sox in 1967; John "Blue Moon" Odom, with the Oakland A's in 1974; and Grant Jackson, with the Pittsburgh Pirates in 1979.

Brooklyn Dodgers and Oakland A's fans will swear that Don Newcombe and Vida Blue also won Series games, but the fact is that neither did. In five World Series appearances, Newcombe had a record of no wins and four losses. Dodger fans might remember a particularly heartbreaking Newcombe loss. In the opening game of the 1949 World Series, the hard-throwing right-hander struck out 11 New York Yankees over the first eight innings, only to give up a home run to "Old Reliable," Tommy Henrich, in the ninth and lose, 1–0.

Vida Blue, in eight Series appearances through 1980, had a record of no wins and three losses.

JOE DIMAGGIO NEVER BUNTED FOR A BASE HIT DURING HIS RECORD-BREAKING 56-GAME HITTING STREAK. WHY?

In an interview with telecaster Warner Wolf, DiMaggio explained that he never bunted because "I was afraid I'd hit myself in the eye. I'd never bunted before. [Yankee manager Joe] McCarthy had never asked me to. He always figured I could go to the opposite field in that situation."

The Baseball Encyclopedia calls DiMaggio's accomplishment "baseball's most amazing single-season hitting streak." During the streak, the Yankee Clipper batted .408 on 91 hits in 223 at bats, including 16 doubles, four triples, 15 home runs, and 55 runs batted in. The streak began on May 15, 1941, and ended on July 16.

ON THE DAY HE PITCHED THE ONLY PERFECT GAME IN WORLD SERIES HISTORY, DON LARSEN ALSO RECEIVED SOME UNPLEASANT NEWS. WHAT WAS IT?

Larsen's wife, Vivian, filed suit charging that he (Larsen) had been delinquent in his support payments (they had been separated) and that he had subjected her and their 14-month-old daughter to "the pleasures of a starvation existence."

WHEN DID A MADISON AVENUE ADVERTISING AGENCY BRING THE NEW YORK YANKEES AND BROOKLYN DODGERS TOGETHER?

On October 1, 1952, an ad for Camel cigarettes appeared in *The New York Times*. The cigarette commercial carried endorsements from nine members of the Dodgers and Yankees, among them Allie Reynolds, Carl Furillo, Billy Cox, and Mickey Mantle. Of Mantle it was said, "Mickey Mantle, youthful star of the Yankees, follows the lead of veteran teammates. He gave Camels a try-out for 30 days and then stayed right with them."

Since the release of the U.S. surgeon-general's warning about cigarette smoking, players have been prohibited from endorsing cigarettes.

THE NEW YORK GIANTS BEAT THE BROOKYLN DODGERS IN THE 1951 BEST-OF-THREE PLAY-OFF ON BOBBY THOMSON'S MIRACLE "SHOT HEARD 'ROUND THE WORLD"—A THREE-RUN HOMERUN OFF RALPH BRANCA. BUT THAT GAME MIGHT NOT HAVE BEEN PLAYED IF A CERTAIN PLAYER HAD NOT HIT A HOME RUN IN THE FIRST GAME THAT PROVIDED THE MARGIN OF VICTORY IN THE GIANT'S 3–1 WIN. NAME

THE PLAYER AND THE PITCHER WHO MADE THE FATEFUL TOSS.

Bobby Thomson hit the home run and Ralph Branca was the pitcher. It happened in the fourth inning of game one, with Brooklyn leading, 1–0. The Dodgers won the second game of the play-off. Had Thomson not hit a home run in the first game, there might never have been a third game.

And, needless to say, no miracle!

JOE DIMAGGIO, TED WILLIAMS, JOE GORDON, KEN KELTNER, CHUCK KLEIN, MEL OTT, AND BABE RUTH ALL HAD ONE THING IN COMMON. WHAT IS IT?

Each player hit as many or more home runs in a single season than an entire team did during that same season. In 1949 Ted Williams hit 43 homers and so did the Chicago White Sox. In 1948 Joe DiMaggio hit 39 and Joe Gordon hit 32, both outproducing the Washington Senators, who hit only 31. In 1936 Mel Ott hit 33 and so did the Brooklyn Dodgers. In 1931 Chuck Klein hit 31, Ott hit 29, and the Cincinnati Reds hit 21. In 1927 Babe Ruth hit 60 and in 1920 he hit 54; incredibly, each year Ruth's home run stats were greater than those of *any other* team.

NAME THE CATCHER WHO CAUGHT A BASEBALL THROWN FROM THE TOP OF THE WASHINGTON MONUMENT.

Gabby Street, a catcher for the Washington Senators in 1908 and 1909. A weak hitter (his highest seasonal average was .238), Street nevertheless was an outstanding catcher, renowned for catching towering pop-fly balls.

One day Pres Gibson, a Washington newspaperman, boasted that Street could catch a ball from any height. A listener wondered if Street could catch a ball falling from as high as 500 feet. "Sure," the reporter said, and they decided the best place for the toss would be the Washington Monument. When informed of the challenge, Street agreed to the stunt.

Gibson himself went to the top of the monument with 13 baseballs. From so high a perch, he could hardly see the catcher standing with the readied glove. At last the moment of truth had arrived. But Gibson's first few tosses caromed wildly in all directions. Finally, on the 13th toss, Street was able to reach the ball, making the catch after the ball had plummeted more than 500 feet.

A RELIEF PITCHER ONCE WAS CALLED TO THE MOUND IN THE FIRST INNING AND THEN PITCHED A PERFECT GAME. WHO WAS HE?

Ernie Shore, a reliever for the Boston Red Sox, turned in one of the finest of relief performances in baseball history on June 23, 1917, in a game against the Washington Senators.

Curiously, the starting pitcher for the Red Sox was a young man named Babe Ruth. However, Ruth got into early trouble, walking the first batter he faced. The Babe believed that several of the pitches should have been called strikes and so informed the umpire. That done, Ruth then punched the umpire in the throat, which resulted in the Babe's instant ejection from the playing field.

Shore was immediately called from the bench and began pitching with very little warm-up. He was told by manager Jake Stahl to simply stall for time because Shore said he had "nothing" that day. After the runner on first was caught trying to steal second, Shore settled down. He pitched perfect baseball for the next 8⅔ innings and was credited with a perfect game, since he was responsible for all 27 outs. No pitcher has ever duplicated this feat.

WHO IS BELIEVED TO HAVE BEEN THE FIRST SALARIED PROFESSIONAL BASEBALL PLAYER?

Lipman Pike, who played with the Athletic Club of Philadelphia in 1866. Pike is considered number one, although Al Reach also claimed that he was first. For many years Reach bragged that he was the game's first pro, and to this day his name can be found on the official American League baseball. However, the printed records of the day (*The Sporting Life of* Philadelphia and *The Sporting News* of St. Louis) agree that Pike was the first to sign, not Reach.

Pike, who was Jewish, also was one of the first stars of the game. Among other accomplishments, he once hit six home runs in one game and was baseball's first long-ball threat. Francis Richter in *Histories and Records of Baseball* observed that "Pike was one of the three best outfielders in baseball during the 1870-1880 era."

WHO WAS THE FIRST PLAYER TO BE DECLARED A FREE AGENT?

In 1937, Tommy Henrich, then Cleveland Indians property, was granted free agency by Baseball Commissioner Kenesaw Mountain Landis. Henrich originally had approached the commissioner when he suspected the Indians had been illegally manipulating his contract. The Commissioner investigated the charge and then granted Henrich free agency. Tommy promptly signed with the New York Yankees for $25,000. As a Yankee, Henrich became known as "Old Reliable," because of his ability to produce in the clutch.

WHO HIT THE FIRST MODERN WORLD SERIES HOME RUN?

Jim Sebring of the Pittsburgh Pirates hit the epochal round tripper, in the opening game of the 1903 World Series. The Pittsburgh Pirates and the Boston Pilgrims were the opponents in the first modern World Series contest. Sebring was the batting star for the Pirates, who nevertheless were defeated, five games to three. In addition to walloping a home run, Sebring batted .367 for the Series.

WHO HIT HOME RUNS IN THE FIRST TWO ALL-STAR GAMES?

St. Louis Cardinals manager and second baseman Frankie Frisch performed the feat in 1933 and 1934. Frisch hit a home run in the first game and followed that up with a homer in the second, only to have his team lose both times. These were the only two All-Star Games in which Frisch appeared.

WHO HIT THE FIRST ALL-STAR GAME HOME RUN?

Appropriately, it was Babe Ruth. El Bambino delivered a two-run blast with Charlie Gehringer on base in the third inning of the first All-Star Game, held on July 6, 1933, at Chicago's Comiskey Park. The American League won the game, 4–2.

HOW MANY HOME RUNS DID FRANK "HOME RUN" BAKER HIT IN HIS MAJOR LEAGUE CAREER?

Home Run Baker hit 93 roundtrippers during his 14-year career. He played for the Philadelphia Athletics from 1908 to 1914. When Connie Mack broke up his famous team in 1914, Baker moved on to the New York Yankees, for whom he played until he retired in 1922.

Baker was a lifetime .307 hitter, but his claim to fame was hitting two home runs in the 1911 World Series to help beat the New York Giants. At the time the two blasts were the most hit by one player in a World Series and remained in the record book for a number of years. Baker led the American League in circuit clouts with 9 in 1911, 10 in 1912, 12 in 1913, and 8 in 1914. He was elected to the Hall of Fame in 1955.

IN THE POST-1900 ERA, ONLY EIGHT BIG-LEAGUERS HAVE HIT OVER .400 IN A REGULAR SEASON; TWO OF THEM DID IT TWICE AND ONE DID IT THREE TIMES. HOW MANY CAN YOU NAME?

1901	Napoleon Lajoie	Philadelphia A's	.422
1911	Joe Jackson	Cleveland Naps	.408
1911	Ty Cobb	Detroit Tigers	.420
1912	Ty Cobb	Detroit Tigers	.410
1920	George Sisler	St. Louis Browns	.407
1922	Ty Cobb	Detroit Tigers	.401
1922	George Sisler	St. Louis Browns	.420
1923	Harry Heilmann	Detroit Tigers	.403
1924	Rogers Hornsby	St. Louis Cards	.424
1925	Rogers Hornsby	St. Louis Cards	.403
1930	Bill Terry	New York Giants	.401
1941	Ted Williams	Boston Red Sox	.406

Napoleon Lajoie, among other accomplishments, enjoyed the unusual distinction of having a team named after him, the Cleveland Naps.

"Shoeless Joe" Jackson, despite his .406 average in 1916, never made it to baseball's Hall of Fame. He was among the conspirators in the notorious Black Sox scandal.

Ty Cobb, who hit .400-plus three times, hammered out 4,191 hits. More than 75 percent of those hits were singles, a by-product of Cobb's extraordinary speed.

Harry Heilmann won batting championships in 1921, 1923, and 1925—and in the even years, he was a tough .350 hitter.

George Sisler broke into the bigs as a pitcher, under Branch Rickey. Before his first at bat, he asked Rickey where he should hit the ball. Amused by the question, Rickey replied: "Try the right-field fence, son." Sisler obliged by hitting the ball over the fence. Rickey got the message and Sisler was moved to first base exclusively. He collected 257 hits in the 1920 campaign, when he batted .407 for the St. Louis Browns.

After batting .401 in 1930, "Memphis Bill" Terry managed the Giants to the 1933 and 1936 National League pennants.

WHAT WAS EDDIE GAEDEL'S CLAIM TO INFAMY IN BIG LEAGUE BASEBALL?

On Sunday, August 19, 1951, Gaedel, a midget wearing number ⅛ on his St. Louis Browns' uniform, took four pitches from Detroit Tigers' pitcher Bob Cain and walked to lead off the second game of a doubleheader at Sportsman's Park, St. Louis. Gaedel, who stood 3'7" and weighed 65 pounds, had batted for substitute center fielder Frank Saucier and was in turn replaced at first by regular center fielder Jimmy Delsing. The Gaedel gambit was the product of promoter Bill Veeck's fertile mind. Veeck owned the Browns at the time.

Frank Saucier, who batted left and threw right, was one of Veeck's top prospects, but he only played 18 games and batted .071 in the majors, all in 1951. Saucier was the only man ever replaced by Gaedel. Delsing, who ran for the midget, spent 12 years in the majors, moving from the Chicago White Sox to the New York Yankees, then to the Browns, to the Tigers, and back to the White Sox, before finally finishing his career, after two years of injury, with the Kansas City A's. He never hit more than .288 as a regular. Neither player was particularly distinguished, but both played a part in one of baseball's more bizarre moments—Saucier being replaced by a midget, and Delsing replacing one.

Commenting on the episode, Veeck said, "This [replacing Saucier] is the only part of the gag I've ever felt bad about. Saucier was a great kid whom I had personally talked back into the game when I bought the Browns. Everything went wrong for Frank, and all he has to show for his great promise is that he was the only guy a midget ever batted for."

Ironically, not only is Gaedel listed in *The Baseball Encyclopedia,* but when he died, *The New York Times* put his obituary on its front page.

NAME THE TWO WORLD SERIES REC-ORDS PETE ROSE HAS TIED.

On October 10, 1970, batting in the fifth inning for the Cincinnati Reds, Rose was awarded first base on catcher's interference when Baltimore Orioles catcher Elrod Hendricks disturbed Rose's swing. Hendricks was given an error by the official scorer and Rose got first on the interference, thus tieing the World Series record for most times awarded first base on a catcher's interference—one.

The other record Rose tied was more admirable.

On October 20, 1972, leading off the game for the Reds, Pete slammed a home run over the right-center field fence, and thus tied the record for most home runs by a leadoff hitter in a World Series game —again, one. Rose circled the bases, never taking his eye off of his victim, Catfish Hunter of the Oakland A's.

Rose holds many records. He has surpassed the

3,000-hit mark and is inching up on Stan Musial's lifetime National League hit mark (3,630). In 1978, he ran up the longest National League hitting streak of the post-1900 era, hitting in 44 consecutive games. Rose also has set major league records for, among other things, highest fielding percentage by an outfielder, lifetime; most seasons with 600 or more at bats; most hits by a switch hitter in a season; most singles by a switch hitter in a season.

WHO WAS THE VERY FIRST MAN EVER TO COME TO BAT IN A WORLD SERIES GAME?

Ginger Beaumont. On October 1, 1903, the Pittsburgh Pirates faced the Boston Pilgrims in the very first World Series between the champions of the National and the American leagues.

Deacon Phillippe of the Pirates, who was 24–9 with a 2.43 earned-run average, was opposed by the venerable Cy Young, then at the peak of his prowess. That year Cy had a 28–9 record and a sparkling 2.08 ERA.

Beaumont, the Pirate center fielder, had hit .341 that year, and his seven home runs tied for the team leadership with Tommy Leach. Beaumont played from 1899 to 1910 and wrapped up his 11-year career with a .311 average, playing most of the years with the Pirates. But he never played in another World Series.

In that historic first at bat, Beaumont flied out to Chuck Stahl, Boston's center fielder, but went on to bat .265 for the Series, going 9 for 34. In that premier game, the first World Series home run was stroked in the seventh inning, by Jimmy Sebring, the

Pirate rightfielder. The Pirates won, 7–3, behind Phillippe. Young took the loss.

In the 1903 Series, Phillippe pitched heroically in five starts, going the distance in all five and picking up three wins and two defeats. The Pilgrims (ancestors of the Red Sox) won the Series, five games to three, in a best-of-nine set.

DO YOU KNOW THE WINNINGEST TEAM OVER A SINGLE SEASON IN BASEBALL HISTORY?

The 1906 Chicago Cubs won 116 and lost only 36, for a remarkable .763 winning percentage.

Their offense was paced by third baseman Harry Steinfeldt, who played in 151 of the Cubs' 154 games, slamming 176 hits to lead the league in that department. He also drove in a league-leading 83 runs and won the batting title with a .327 mark. Steinfeldt made himself equally visible at the hot corner, taking part in more double-plays than the famed Tinker-Evers-Chance combination of the Chicago Cubs and leading the league in fielding.

Despite their hitting prowess, the 1906 Cubs were defeated in the World Series by the Chicago White Sox, the famed "Hitless Wonders," who had not a single .300 hitter in their line-up.

The Cubs also boasted the top three ERA pitchers in the National League, all of whom recorded marks of 1.65 or lower. Three-Finger Brown, a magnificent artist on the mound, led the staff with a 1.04 ERA and 26 wins. Five pitchers had ERAs under 2.00, and none had over 2.21. A phenomenal club.

HOW DID A DROPPED THIRD STRIKE CONTRIBUTE TO THE DETROIT TIGERS' DEFEAT AT THE HANDS OF THE CHICAGO CUBS IN THE 1907 WORLD SERIES?

In the bottom of the ninth inning of the opening game, the Cubs were trailing, 3–1. On the mound for Detroit was Wild Bill Donovan, a 24-game winner that season. Frank Chance, the Cubs' leadoff hitter, singled to right field. Donovan then beaned Harry Steinfeldt, bringing the tying run to the plate. Johnny Kling, who represented that run, promptly bunted to first baseman Claude Rossman, who caught the ball easily on the fly. Johnny Evers then hit a grounder to third baseman Bill Coughlin, who couldn't get a handle on it, and the bases were loaded with only one out.

Cubs manager Frank Chance then called upon Del Howard to pinch-hit for weak-hitting Joe Tinker, but Howard struck out. But Tiger catcher Boss Schmidt dropped the ball, and Howard hustled safely to first while Chance and Steinfeldt scored to tie up the game.

The deadlock remained until the 12th inning, when the game was called because of darkness. The Tigers were demoralized by the Cubs' comeback—not to mention the National Leaguers' seven stolen bases during the game—and subsequently collapsed, losing the next four in a row.

Even Detroit fans sensed that their Tigers were going to lose. The combined attendance for the two games in Detroit was 18,676—in a 40,000-seat stadium. Apart from the psychological advantage gained by Schmidt's *faux pas,* the Cubs benefited from a record 18 stolen bases.

WHAT DETROIT TIGER PITCHER PRO-
DUCED A REMARKABLE 2.60 EARNED-RUN
AVERAGE BUT FINISHED THE SEASON WITH
NOTHING BETTER THAN A .500 RECORD?

George Mullin of the Tigers produced an unusual
20–20 record in 1907, starting 42 games and completing 35. Mullin did improve his statistics. In 1908 he
won 24 and lost 12 with a 1.94 ERA. In 1909 he won
29 and lost nine with a 2.22 ERA, to lead the league
in winning percentage and in wins.

"Wabash George," who was born on July 4, 1880,
also played second base and the outfield. In 1913 he
suffered a terrible year. He jumped to the Federal
League in 1914 and concluded his career with the
"Feds." He had a lifetime record of 229–191.

Pitchers who win 20 or more and lose 20 or more
in the same season are not that rare. The Atlanta
Braves' Phil Niekro, for example, won 21 and lost 20
in 1979. Speaking of remarkable records, how about
Joel Horlen's 2.43 ERA with the Chicago White Sox
in 1966 when his record was 10–13. That same year
Gary Peters of the White Sox produced a 1.98 ERA
and a 12–10 record. In 1978 Steve Rogers of the
Montreal Expos had a 2.45 ERA and an 11–13 record.
He was beaten by Craig Swan of the New York Mets
who had a 2.43 ERA and a 9–6 record.

DID BABE RUTH MAKE HIS FIRST WORLD
SERIES APPEARANCE WITH THE NEW YORK
YANKEES OR THE BOSTON RED SOX?

Prior to becoming a Yankee, Ruth was an excellent pitcher with the Red Sox. In 1915 he posted a
2.44 earned-run average and an 18–6 record in 28

starts and 32 games. But Red Sox manager Bill Carrigan hesitated to employ the Babe in World Series play that year because he believed that as a rookie, Ruth was too inexperienced to take a regular turn against the Philadelphia Phillies. In the opener, however, Ruth was called upon to pinch-hit for pitcher Ernie Shore. Babe grounded out to first baseman Fred Luderus, moving teammate Olaf Henriksen to second. The next batter, Harry Hooper, popped to Luderus to end the ball game.

Babe's home runs came later.

IN WHICH WORLD SERIES DID A TEAM USE A TOTAL OF ONLY 11 PLAYERS AND *STILL WIN THE SERIES?*

In 1910 the Philadelphia Athletics walked off with the pennant by winning 102 games and finishing 14½ games in front of the nearest opposition, the New York Highlanders. Prior to the World Series the A's were tormented with injuries and found themselves with only 11 able-bodied players, although not all the injured were on the disabled list.

The A's excellent pitching staff of Jack Coombs, Chief Bender, Eddie Plank, and Cy Morgan was cut in half, only Bender and Coombs remaining. The other pitchers were sore-armed or unreliable. And Coombs, despite his 1.30 earned-run average and 31 wins, had given up 115 walks, second in the league. Chief Bender, who relied on his brains more than his brawn, had the highest winning percentage in the league, with a 23–5 record.

Connie Mack's aces were equally short of fielders, six of whom were forced to ride the bench. As it happened, the A's only had nine nonpitchers available for duty. Nevertheless, the A's prevailed in the Series, beating the Cubs in five games.

In the opener, Chief Bender outlasted Orval Overall, winning 4–1 on hits by Frank Baker; the Chief allowed only three hits. The second game matched Jack Coombs against Three-Finger Brown. Coombs went the distance and Philadelphia won, 9–3. The A's got four doubles in the seventh inning in that romp.

After a day off for travel, Coombs was asked to pitch the third game on only one day's rest. Yet he won again, 12–5, pitching a complete game, with Frank Baker again leading the way in the batting department. In the fourth game, Chief Bender lost to King Cole and Three-Finger Brown (in relief) in a 4–3 thriller that the Cubs won in the bottom of the ninth with two outs.

Coombs took the mound for game five with two days rest and went the distance again, beating Three-Finger Brown, 7–2. Coombs had pitched three games, compiling a 3–0 record and a 3.33 ERA and striking out 17, Bender pitched two, winning one and finishing with a 1.93 ERA. The A's got their hitting from the eight starters, four of whom batted over .350. Eddie Collins was tops at .429.

WHO WON THE LONGEST GAME (BY NUMBER OF INNINGS) IN WORLD SERIES PLAY?

In 1916 the Brooklyn Robins (later to be known as the Brooklyn Dodgers), won their first pennant since 1900. The Robins were composed primarily of

41

castoffs from other clubs. Chief Meyers, Rube Marquard, and Fred Merkle had played for the New York Giants, and Jack Coombs had come over from the Philadelphia Athletics. Other Dodger stars included Casey Stengel and Zack Wheat, who hammered out 17 home runs between them, an unusually high number in those dead-ball days.

The Brooklyn nine met the Boston Red Sox in the 1916 World Series. The veteran Bosox boasted Harry Hooper, Ernie Shore, Dutch Leonard, Carl Mays, and Rube Foster, among other stars, and they also had Babe Ruth, then a crackerjack pitcher.

In the second game, Ruth was opposed by southpaw Sherry Smith of Brooklyn. In the regular season Ruth had had a 23–12 record and a 1.75 earned-run average, including nine shutouts, while Smith had chalked up a 2.34 ERA and a 17–10 record. The Robins scored a run in the first inning but the Red Sox tied it at 1–1 in the third. From there on it was a pitcher's classic, as Ruth and Smith each allowed but four hits.

The Sox came close to ending the game in the ninth, when leadoff hitter Hal Janvrin doubled and Brooklyn third baseman Mike Mowrey dropped a grounder, allowing runners on first and third. But the rally was cut short when Sox first baseman Dick Hoblitzell lined to Myers in center and Myers nailed Janvrin at the plate for a double play. The inning ended when Larry Gardner fouled out to catcher Otto Miller.

The score remained tied going into the bottom half of the 14th inning, when Hoblitzell, leading off, drew his fourth walk of the game. Left fielder Duffy Lewis sacrificed Hoblitzell to second, whereupon Mike McNally was sent in to run for Hoblitzell. Del Gainer was ordered to hit for third baseman Larry

Gardner and singled to right, sending McNally home with the winning run, two hours and 32 minutes after the game had started.

Babe Ruth had gone the distance, as had Sherry Smith, in the longest game in World Series history.

The Robins won the next game behind Jack Coombs but lost the Series to Boston, four games to one.

The irony of the game is that the two hours and 32 minutes needed to play the 14 innings did not set a new Series record for game length by time. The longest game to that point was a three-hour-and-six-minute battle in 1914 that went only 12 innings!

WHEN DID THE FIRST WORLD SERIES GRAND SLAM AND ONLY WORLD SERIES UNASSISTED TRIPLE PLAY TAKE PLACE?

On October 10, 1920, in Cleveland, the Indians' fans were treated to a display of World Series histrionics.

In the very first inning of the fifth game, Cleveland left fielder Charlie Jamieson singled to lead off. Bill Wambsganss, the second baseman, followed with a short single. Tris Speaker then beat out a bunt, loading the bases for Elmer Smith, the center fielder, who hit .316 that year, along with 12 home runs.

Opposing the Indians were the Brooklyn Robins; the teams were tied in the Series at two games apiece. On the mound for the Robins was spitballer Burleigh Grimes. Smith slammed the ball over the right field fence and screen to put the Indians in front, 4–0, in the first inning with no one out.

By the end of four innings the Indians were

leading, 7–0. Starting off the top of the fifth, Pete Kilduff hit a leadoff single for the Robins. This was followed by a single off the bat of catcher Otto Miller. That brought up the Robins' pitcher, Clarence Mitchell, with runners on first and second and none out. Mitchell hit, a liner that was flagged down by second baseman Bill Wambsganss (for one), who then stepped on second (for two) and finally touched the baserunning Miller for the third out. This was accomplished in about three motions.

WHEN DID BOTH TEAMS SHARE A SINGLE HOME STADIUM IN THE WORLD SERIES?

The early 1920s saw the emergence of the New York Yankees as the preeminent team in baseball. But the Yanks won their first pennants before the new Yankee Stadium was completed in 1923. While the stadium was under construction, the Yankees won pennants in 1921 and 1922, playing "home" games at the Polo Grounds, in Manhattan—the home of the New York Giants.

John Brush and John McGraw, owner and manager, respectively, of the then-mighty Giants, discounted the Yankees as serious threats to their fans until Babe Ruth came along. Meanwhile, Yankee owner Jacob Ruppert built his new baseball palace across the Harlem River.

The Giants and Yankees each won pennants in 1921, 1922, and 1923 with the 1921 and 1922 Series taking place at the Polo Grounds and the teams alternating as home and visitor. The opener, on October 5, 1921, saw the Giants at home. In the second game the Giants were visitors. There were no off days, except Sunday, when baseball was prohibited because of the New York blue laws.

The shared-stadium routine took place again in 1944 when the Browns and Cardinals played the World Series at their home Sportsman's Park in St. Louis.

The Giants won both World Series at the Polo Grounds—the 1921 Series, five games to three, the 1922 Series, four games to none, with one disputed tie. That came in the second game, when the Giants had their 3-0 lead chipped to a tie in the tenth. In an overcautious moment, the umpires called the game because of darkness, although it didn't turn dark for another 45 minutes. Enraged fans immediately blamed the innocent Baseball Commissioner Kenesaw Mountain Landis. Landis finally agreed to turn over the gate receipts to New York hospitals for disabled veterans.

By the time the 1923 World Series came around, Yankee Stadium had been completed and the two teams traveled back and forth between the Polo Grounds and Yankee Stadium. The Yanks won that Series, four games to two.

WHAT MISCUES BECAME THE BANE OF FRED LINDSTROM'S LIFE?

In the 1924 World Series between the New York Giants and the Washington Senators, the Giants led, 3-1, in the bottom of the eighth inning in the final game of the Series. The Senators were at bat when, with one away, Nemo Leibold doubled down the third-base line. Muddy Ruel followed with a single off first baseman George Kelly's glove, moving Leibold to third. Pinch hitter Bennie Tate was walked and replaced by pinch runner Mule Shirley. Although Giants pitcher Virgil Barnes was in serious trouble, he got Earl McNeely to fly to left field, the runners holding. Now, with two outs, Bucky Harris, the Senators' player-manager, hit a grounder that bounced on a pebble in front of Giants' rookie third baseman Fred Lindstrom. The ball hopped up, eluded the frustrated Lindstrom, and headed for left field. Lindstrom remained motionless while two runs scored, tying the game. Barnes was removed in favor of Art Nehf, who retired the side.

The Senators having tied the game, brought in veteran Walter Johnson as a reliever to start the ninth. The Big Train held the Giants in check until the bottom of the 12th, when, with one out, Muddy Ruel lifted an ordinarily easy pop foul. But Giants catcher Hank Gowdy stepped on his mask, tripped, and missed the pop-up, giving Ruel life. Muddy immediately doubled past third base. Walter Johnson reached first on an error, whereupon Earl McNeely rapped an apparently easy out in the direction of Lindstrom. But the ball bounced off a piece of clay and, again, jumped over Lindstrom's head, scoring the Series-winning run for the Senators.

Eventually, Lindstrom redeemed himself. He enjoyed a 12-year major league career at third base, hammering out a .311 lifetime average—including .358 in 1928 and .379 in 1930. He was a power hitter for the Giants until 1932, then for the Pirates, the Cubs, and the Dodgers. He was elected to the Hall of Fame in 1976. But his inability to handle several grounders in the 1924 World Series overshadowed most of his positive feats.

That Series, incidentally, was John McGraw's

last as Giants manager. The Giants were not a contender after 1924, despite the presence of such sluggers as Lindstrom, Bill Terry, and Mel Ott.

By contrast, the 1924 World Series proved to be Walter Johnson's finest hour. The Senators' one and only World Series victory was spearheaded by Johnson's three-hit no-run, four-inning stint in the final game, which proved that the old master was not washed up—as many suspected after he had lost the opener.

HOW DID THE PHILADELPHIA ATHLETICS OVERCOME AN EIGHT-RUN DEFICIT IN THE SEVENTH INNING OF THE FOURTH GAME OF THE 1929 WORLD SERIES TO WIN THE CONTEST FROM THE CHICAGO CUBS?

Chicago pitcher Charlie Root was coasting along with an 8-0 shutout when Al Simmons led off the bottom half of the seventh for the Athletics. Simmons, who boasted a .365 batting average that year, with 34 home runs and a towering 157 runs batted in, was in vintage form. He smashed a home run onto the roof of the Stadium's left field stands. The score was now 8-1, Chicago.

This brought up Jimmy Foxx, a man who hit 33 homers that year, along with a sizzling .354 batting average and 117 runs batted in. Foxx singled to right field. That was followed by a single from Bing Miller, which was lost in the sun by veteran Hack Wilson as Foxx sped to third. Jimmy Dykes also singled, scoring Foxx and moving Miller to second. The score was now 8-2, Chicago. Next, Joe Boley singled for the fifth consecutive Philadelphia hit, scoring Miller. The score now was 8-3, Chicago.

Connie Mack, the A's manager, knew a good thing when he saw it. He yanked his pitcher, Ed Rommel, and sent George Burns in to pinch-hit. Burns popped up for the first out. One down. But Max Bishop followed with a bloop single. Another run scored, and now it was 8–4, Chicago, with two on and one out.

That was enough for Cubs manager Joe McCarthy. He yanked Charlie Root and replaced him with Art Nehf, who had a 5.58 earned-run average and an 8–5 record. Nehf took his warmup tosses and then faced Mule Haas, who proceeded to belt a hard line drive that Hack Wilson lost in the sun as it went by him to the wall. By the time Wilson retrieved the ball and fired it home, Hass had a three-run, inside-the-park home run. The score was now 8–7, and the fans were on their feet, screaming.

Mickey Cochrane, the great Athletics' catcher, was walked. McCarthy gave Nehf the hook and replaced him with Sheriff Blake, who was 14–13 with a 4.20 earned-run average. Blake allowed Al Simmons (the A's now had batted around) a single over third sacker Norm MacMillan's head, Cochrane reaching second. Jimmy Foxx then singled again, and the ball game was tied, 8–8.

Enraged, McCarthy brought in his ace, Pat Malone, who had a 22–10 record with a 3.57 ERA. Malone was wild and immediately hit Bing Miller to load the bases. McCarthy stayed with Malone, whereupon Jimmy Dykes slammed a double to the left-field wall. Simmons and Foxx scored to make it 10–8, A's. At last, Malone disposed of Boley and Burns, the pinch hitter coming up for his second at bat. The final score was 10–8, A's. Philadelphia won the Series in five games.

WHO LOST THE MOST GAMES (LIFE-TIME) IN WORLD SERIES PLAY?

Whitey Ford of the New York Yankees held a number of World Series records, the most notable of them being his pitching 33⅔ scoreless innings consecutively. But he also lost eight Series games—a record.

Ford also started the most World Series games (22), a tribute to his longevity and the Yankees' ability to get into the Fall Classic. He pitched three shutouts as part of his consecutive-scoreless-inning record. Whitey gave up the most walks (34), struck out a record 94 batters, hurled a record 146 innings, pitched seven complete games, and won 10 of the World Series games he pitched.

Other big losers were Bullet Joe Bush, Christy Mathewson, Eddie Plank, and Schoolboy Rowe, each of whom lost five Series games.

Ford's eight losses actually were a tribute to his ability, since he was entrusted with the ball in so many games. Whitey pitched his way to a decision in all but four of his World Series starts.

WHY WAS ACCLAIMED SLUGGER DUCKY MEDWICK THROWN OUT OF THE FINAL GAME OF THE 1934 WORLD SERIES BETWEEN THE ST. LOUIS CARDINALS AND THE DETROIT TIGERS?

The Cardinals had a seven-run third inning during the seventh game, which gave them a 7–0 lead. By the sixth inning, the Cardinals were ahead by 11–0, and the hometown Tiger fans were growing angry and increasingly restless. The visiting Cardinals were making the Bengals look like minor leaguers.

In the top of the sixth inning, Joe "Ducky" Medwick, the .319-hitting St. Louis left fielder, hit a triple—his first of the Series—and finished the play by sliding hard into third baseman Marv Owen.

Medwick's triple was not surprising, since he had smacked 18 to lead the National League in three-baggers that year. But it was the last straw for the Tigers' fans, particularly when Joe wrestled briefly with Owen in an effort to beat the tag and get to his feet. Briggs Stadium was in an uproar when the Cardinals finally were retired, still leading 11–0.

When Medwick ran out to left field to start the bottom of the sixth, he was pelted with garbage, bottles, fruit, and assorted debris. To avoid injury, Medwick wandered off to second base while the groundskeeper cleaned the field.

When Ducky returned, the fans bombarded him again, this time with increased vigor. Baseball Commissioner Kenesaw Mountain Landis summoned St. Louis manager Frankie Frisch and ordered Medwick's removal from the game. Medwick reluctantly departed in favor of Chick Fullis. The Cardinals won, 11–0, to take the Series in seven games.

WHEN THE INIMITABLE LOU GEHRIG RETIRED FROM THE NEW YORK YANKEES, WHO WAS CHOSEN TO FILL HIS SHOES AT FIRST BASE?

Gehrig was replaced by rookie Babe Dahlgren in the 1939 season, after Gehrig had played in his record 2,130 games.

Dahlgren was not a power hitter, but he did

50

produce 15 home runs in his first year, as well as 89 runs batted in. Dahlgren's average was a mediocre .235. Surrounded by such mighty hitters as Joe DiMaggio, Bill Dickey, and Charlie Keller, Dahlgren was relegated to hitting eighth in the Yankees batting order.

The Yankees eventually shipped Dahlgren to the Braves in 1941 and elevated the promising Johnny Sturm to replace him. Dahlgren went from the Braves to the Cubs, the Browns, the Phillies, the Pirates, and then back to the Browns, before he retired in 1946. Babe's lifetime batting average was .261. He hit a total of 82 home runs. Dahlgren's claim to fame is the fact that when Gehrig asked to be taken out of the lineup on May 8, 1939, he took over.

WHO WON THE 1945 ALL-STAR GAME?
Nobody. Because so many genuine All-Stars had gone to war, Baseball Commissioner Happy Chandler cancelled the traditional midsummer fête, replacing it with exhibition contests played by major league teams against minor league clubs, military clubs, and college teams. The proceeds were diverted to the war effort. The All-Star Game was reinstated in 1946, when the American League defeated the National League, 12–0, at Fenway Park in Boston.

CAN YOU NAME THE FAMOUS PITCHER WHO *LOST* THE MOST GAMES, LIFETIME?
Cy Young, after whom the most-valuable-pitcher award is named, holds a number of records—906

career appearances, the majority of them starts (816); 750 complete games, again a record; a total 7,357 innings pitched, yet another record. Young is number one in wins, with 511, but also number one in losses, with 313.

Young's awesome number of complete games pitched gave him a hefty amount of decisions, and despite his great control, he could not win all of them. In those days before relief specialists, Young would pitch at least every other day, sometimes every day, and occasionally both ends of a doubleheader during his stewardship with Cleveland, St. Louis, and Boston. Young's losses also are a measure of the managers' confidence in him. Even in losing battles it was a rare day when anyone pinch-hit for Cy Young.

WHAT WAS THE STARTING LINEUP FOR THE ST. LOUIS BROWNS IN 1944, THE ONE AND ONLY YEAR THEY WON AN AMERICAN LEAGUE PENNANT?

The Brownies, the flubs of many a decade, enjoyed their brief season in the sun during World War II.

In 1944, with most rosters decimated by the war, the onetime powerhouses were rendered impotent. The New York Yankees, for example, put 45-year-old Paul Waner in center field because Joe DiMaggio was serving in the Coast Guard. That season, however, the St. Louis Browns came into their own, outdistancing the Detroit Tigers and the Yankees in the homestretch. To do so the Browns swept a doubleheader on the last day of the season from the equally ravaged Washington Senators, thus nosing out the

Tigers for the pennant. In the World Series the St. Louis Cardinals, who were able to hang onto a corps of veterans and stars, beat the Browns, four games to two.

The Browns had 35-year-old George McQuinn at first base. McQuinn hit .250, with 11 home runs. In the World Series, he hit .438.

At second was Don Gutteridge, who stole 20 bases, hit .245, and stroked three home runs.

The shortstop was Vern Stephens, who led the league with 109 runs batted in, stroked 20 home runs and batted .293.

Mark Christman, who played third, hit .271 that year, with six home runs and 47 RBIs. He was 34 at the time of the Brownies' pennant.

The right fielder was 35-year-old Gene Moore. In 1944 he hit .238 and had six homers. He was known as "Rowdy" for his incessant bench-jockeying.

Center fielder Mike Kreevich, age 34, in the twilight of his career, hit .301 and got five home runs. In 1945 both Moore and Kreevich would retire.

Rounding out the fielders was veteran Brownie Chet Laabs, who hit only .234, with five home runs.

The Browns' catcher was Red Hayworth, a 29-year-old rookie who hit a lowly .223 and had only one home run. He played one more season, dropped his average to .194, and then retired.

The pitching staff was led by 34-year-old Jack Kramer, who was 17–13, with a 2.49 earned-run average and 124 strikeouts. It was his best year.

For Sig Jackucki, 1944 was the first time in eight years he had pitched in the majors. Wartime shortages brought him in, and he functioned well, going 13 and nine, with a 3.55 ERA. He retired the next year, at age 35.

Bob Muncrief, the third starter, went 13 and eight, with a 3.08 ERA. He was 28, and tooled around the majors for 12 years, departing in 1951.

Nelson Potter, age 34, won 19 and lost seven, with a 2.83 ERA. Nels pitched for six teams over 14 years with indifferent results.

The fireman of the club was George Caster, whose 12 saves led the American League. At 37, he was still able to compile a 2.44 ERA, and a 6–6 record, entirely in relief.

The Brownies were a collection of aged veterans, young kids, and dregs, but they did win an American League pennant in 1944—their only one ever.

THREE KEY PARTICIPANTS IN THE 1947 WORLD SERIES NEVER PLAYED ANOTHER BIG LEAGUE GAME. CAN YOU REMEMBER ANY OF THEIR NAMES?

The New York Yankees and the Brooklyn Dodgers were hot rivals by 1947. In the fourth game of the World Series, Bill Bevens of the Bombers and Harry Taylor of the Brooks squared off at Ebbets Field.

Taylor was quickly knocked out and replaced by Hal Gregg. But Bevens rolled mightly along, giving up ten walks, a wild pitch, and one run—*but not allowing a single hit* through eight innings.

In the bottom of the ninth, Carl Furillo of the Dodgers was walked with one out. Al Gionfriddo was sent in to run for Furillo. With two out, relief pitcher Hugh Casey departed in favor of pinch hitter Pistol Pete Reiser, who was suffering from a lame ankle. Reiser was intentionally walked to bring up weak-hitting Eddie Stanky. But Stanky never made it to the mound. He was replaced by ancient third baseman, Cookie Lavagetto. Lavagetto responded with a line drive that bounced off the right-field wall to score Gionfriddo as well as Eddie Miksis, who had been sent in to run for Reiser. Lavagetto's double won the game for Brooklyn, 3–2. Bevens had lost a no-hitter as well as a World Series one-hitter, in the bottom of the ninth.

Although both appeared again in the course of the Series, neither Bevens nor Lavagetto would ever play in another regular-season game. Bevens had had a bad year and decided to conclude his four-year career after the Series. Lavagetto was winding down a 14-year career, ten of them with the Dodgers. He packed it in with a .300 lifetime average.

Gionfriddo, the third man in the group, also starred in the crucial sixth game at Yankee Stadium. With two on and two out in the bottom of the sixth, Joe DiMaggio lifted a fly ball that appeared to be a sure home run in left field, until Gionfriddo flagged it down at the 415-foot sign in front of the bullpen. As the stoical DiMaggio rounded second, he saw the ball slam into Gionfriddo's glove. The Yankee Clipper then betrayed emotion for one of the few times in his career, kicking at the dirt before returning to the bench. The catch saved the sixth game and kept Dodger hurler Joe Hatten alive.

Gionfriddo was concluding a four-year major-league career, including stints in Pittsburgh and Brooklyn. In 37 games with the Brooks in 1947 he hit .177. He did no better in Pittsburgh before he arrived in Brooklyn, playing one game and hitting .000.

Gionfriddo's catch kept the Dodgers alive and helped them tie the Series. He was never heard from again. Gionfriddo, Bevens, and Lavagetto saw their names inscribed in the books and then departed from the scene.

WHO WERE THE ONLY TWO MEN TO APPEAR IN UNIFORM IN THE ONLY TWO AMERICAN LEAGUE PLAY-OFF GAMES (DISCOUNTING THE CURRENT DIVISIONAL SYSTEM)?

On October 4, 1948, Bob Lemon, the Cleveland Indians' pitcher who had completed the regular season with a 20–14 record and a 2.82 earned-run average, sat in the dugout watching teammate Gene Bearden down the Boston Red Sox, 8–3, in the first American League play-off. Bearden started against the Red Sox rather than Lemon because he had a 20–7 season and a league leading 2.43 earned-run average—excellent credentials for a rookie.

Playing third base and batting second for the Red Sox that day was Johnny Pesky. The ever-dependable Pesky had given Red Sox fans brief visions of a "trolley series" (Boston's other team, the Braves, had won the National League pennant) when he doubled and scored to knot the game at 1–1. But Cleveland came back to win the game and went on to win the World Series four games to two. The winning pitcher in the last game of the series was Bob Lemon.

On October 3, 1978, 30 years less a day after the first American League play-off, Bob Lemon and Johnny Pesky were adversaries again in a playoff situation. This time both players were on the sidelines, Lemon in Yankee pinstripes managing the team, and

Pesky working the first base coaching box for the Red Sox.

The Yankees won 5–4 and for the second time Lemon went on to more championship play while Pesky returned home for the winter.

As a manager, Lemon had piloted the Yankees to a successful comeback after they had been, at one time, 14 games out of first place.

The Yanks won the play-off game on Bucky Dent's home run in the seventh inning and Rich Gossage's blazing fastballs in the eighth and ninth.

Curiously, both play-offs were held in Fenway Park and both were won by a team that had come from behind that year and not been considered a threat in midseason. Both winning teams (Indians and Yanks) were visitors. Similarly, both the Yankees of 1978 and the Indians of 1948 had pitchers with outstanding seasons—Guidry, Gossage, and Ed Figueroa for the Yanks; Bearden, Lemon, and Bob Feller for Cleveland. Both had two reliable hitters—Graig Nettles and Reggie Jackson for the Yanks; Joe Gordon and Ken Keltner for the Tribe.

The Indians catcher of 1948, Jim Hegan later would become a Yankee coach. And the Tribe's left fielder, .336-hitting Dale Mitchell, would play an important role in Yankee history, although not as a Yankee: Mitchell was the last batter Don Larsen faced when he pitched his perfect World Series game against the Brooklyn Dodgers on October 8, 1956.

WHO WERE THE "WHIZ KIDS" OF BIG-LEAGUE BASEBALL?

The 1950 Philadelphia Phillies won the National

League pennant by beating the Brooklyn Dodgers on the final day of the season, in extra innings on Dick Sisler's home run. The Phils were dubbed Whiz Kids because of their wealth of starry young talent, including Richie Ashburn, Del Ennis, Willie Jones, and Robin Roberts.

The fleet Ashburn, who became the Phillies' star center fielder for years to come, batted .303 that year and led the National League in triples with an eye-opening 14.

Right fielder Ennis led the National League in runs batted in with 126, hit .311, and hammered 31 homers.

Sisler's home run, which dispatched the Phillies into the World Series, was a rare shot for a man who hit only four roundtrippers that season and only 55 in his 20-year major league career.

Seminick, the Phils' catcher, hit 24 homers and batted .288.

Granny Hamner, the shortstop, hit .270 with 11 homers.

Willie Jones, the third baseman, hit 25 homers, along with 88 RBIs.

Jim Konstanty established himself as the National League's foremost relief pitcher, and the first of the modern bullpen artists. He amassed 22 saves and had a 16–7 record, without a start. Konstanty, at 33, was the elder statesman of the Whiz Kids.

The Phillies' premier pitcher was 24-year-old Robin Roberts, who led the league in starts with 39, won 20 and lost 11, and notched a 3.99 ERA.

The Phillies won the pennant with a distillation of power and speed. But in the World Series they were routed in four straight by the Yankees, who only allowed three earned runs while holding the Philly bats to a lowly .203 average.

The Yankee machine was too much for the Whiz Kids.

IN WHICH WORLD SERIES DID TEN FUTURE BIG LEAGUE MANAGERS PLAY?

The 1951 classic featuring the New York Yankees and the New York Giants.

Among the players participating was Billy Martin who appeared as a pinch runner. As a manager, he would lead the Detroit Tigers to a division title and the Minnesota Twins to the top of their division twice, put the Texas Rangers into contention, and in his finest and most controversial hour, manage the Yankees to two consecutive pennants and a world championship before being fired in 1978. He would later be rehired to finish the Yankees' dismal 1979 season. The Yankees fired him again that winter and in 1980 Billy managed the Oakland Athletics. He guided the previously inept A's to a remarkable second place finish and as a result was runner up to Houston's Bill Virdon in both The Sporting News and UPI's manager of the year polls.

Another veteran of the 1951 series was Hank Bauer, the ex-marine on the Yankees, who hit in 17 Series games in a row but was held to a .167 average in the 1951 Series. Bauer would lead the Yankees in the 1958 World Series and eventually manage the Baltimore Orioles to the pennant and a World Series sweep over the Los Angeles Dodgers in 1966.

Jerry Coleman, the spare second baseman of the Yankees in 1951, became a sportscaster for the Yanks and later for the San Diego Padres. In 1979 he was summoned from the press booth to the dugout by Padres' owner Ray Kroc, who then turned around and fired Coleman after the 1980 season.

Yogi Berra, the Yankees first-string catcher in 1951, hit .261 in the '51 Series. He later managed both the Yankees (1964) and the Mets (1973) and led both to a pennant and to a seven-game World Series, only to fail in the seventh game both times and get fired thereafter.

Eddie Lopat, the Yankee pitcher who won two complete games against the Giants with "junk" pitches, went on to manage the Kansas City Athletics in 1963 and 1964.

The New York Giants of 1951 had no shortage of managing potential either. First baseman Whitey Lockman, who batted .282 in 1951, managed the Chicago Cubs from 1972 to 1974. Whitey replaced his former boss, Leo Durocher, in the middle of the '72 season and the Cubs finished second, behind the deadly Pittsburgh Pirates. The next year the Cubs fell apart, slipping to fifth place in the National League's Eastern Division. Lockman was fired in the middle of the 1974 campaign as his team fell to last place, losing 97 games.

Alvin Dark, who led the National League in doubles (41) in 1951, later managed the Giants and several other teams. He led the Giants to the 1962 pennant and took the Athletics' helm in 1966. He lasted two years there and moved on to Cleveland for three years. Dark won a pennant and a World Series in his first year (1974) with the Oakland A's. Dark managed the A's for two more years, taking the division in 1975. The owner Charlie Finley broke up the dissension-riddled club, and Dark departed.

Wes Westrum, the Giants' catcher who belted 20 homers in 1951, managed the Mets for two years (1966 and 1967), replacing Casey Stengel.

Bill Rigney, another alumnus of the 1951 Giants, replaced Leo Durocher as Giants manager in 1956 and managed them until 1960, when he was replaced by former teammate Alvin Dark. Rigney later managed the California Angels until 1969. He moved on to the Minnesota Twins and led them to a play-off in 1970. Rigney returned to the Giants in 1976 and then retired.

Eddie Stanky, who drew 127 walks and hit .247 with the '51 Giants, managed the Cardinals from 1953 to 1955. He then managed in the minors before returning to the majors as boss of the Chicago White Sox from 1966 to 1968.

Finally, a word for Ralph Houk, the Yankees third-string catcher in 1951. Houk spent the '51 Series warming up pitchers in the Yanks' bullpen. He managed the Yanks for a number of years (1961–63; 1969–75) and finished up with the Detroit Tigers (1977–79).

HOW DID BILLY MARTIN SAVE THE NEW YORK YANKEES FROM DEFEAT IN THE 1952 WORLD SERIES?

In the seventh and deciding game of the 1952 Fall Classic, held at Ebbets Field, the Yanks were leading the Brooklyn Dodgers, 4–2, going into the bottom of the seventh inning, with the Dodgers coming to bat. Yankee manager Casey Stengel sent in Joe Collins as a defensive measure to replace veteran John Mize at first base and called upon Vic Raschi to pitch in relief of Allie Reynolds, who had earlier supplanted starter Eddie Lopat.

The Dodgers' Rocky Nelson, a reliable pinch hitter, batted for pitcher Preacher Roe and popped up for one out. Right fielder Carl Furillo then walked. Third baseman Billy Cox followed with a single to right, moving Furillo to second. Brooklyn now had two on with one out and the go-ahead run, short-stop Pee Wee Reese, coming to bat. Reese walked, loading the bases.

Center fielder Duke Snider moved in to the bat-ter's box, whereupon Stengel removed Raschi in favor of reliever Bob Kuzava. Kuzava got Snider to pop up to third baseman Gil McDougald. With two out, the runners would all be in motion as Jackie Robinson stepped to the plate. Kuzava was sharp and forced Robinson to lift a short fly along the right side, one that first baseman Joe Collins seemed ready to nab. But then Collins lost the ball in the late-afternoon sun as Furillo and Cox headed for home.

Suddenly Martin, the Yankees young second baseman, sped from his "in" position, raced for the ball and gloved it around the knees without breaking stride. Martin kept running, reaching the dugout with the ball still held firmly in his mitt. The Dodgers' rally was snuffed out and Kuzava stopped them the rest of the way. The final score was Yankees 4, Dodgers 2.

Martin later claimed that he was unaware of the significance of his catch until he saw game films later.

HALL OF FAMER WILLIE MAYS WAS RE-NOWNED FOR HIS MARVELOUS FIELDING, BUT ONE CATCH ABOVE ALL IS CONSIDERED

WILLIE'S BEST. WHO HIT THE BALL AND HOW DID MAYS CATCH IT?

The catch was made during the eighth inning of the first game of the 1954 World Series between Mays' New York Giants and the Cleveland Indians. The batter was Vic Wertz, who had been acquired from Baltimore late in the 1954 season to help spell Dale Mitchell and had batted .275. On September 29, he whacked a fly ball off Giants pitcher Don Liddle to the deepest part of center field in the Polo Grounds. Normally such a clout would be a sure triple, and with runners on first and second and none out a rally seemed in the offing. But Mays turned his back to the ball, galloped toward the wall, and snared the fly with an over-the-shoulder catch.

The catch changed the situation entirely and effectively extinguished the Indians' rally. The Giants won the game, 5–2, and went on to beat Cleveland in a four-game sweep.

Hard-luck Wertz hit .500 during the Series, but in a losing cause. He had a 16-year career in the majors with the Detroit Tigers, St. Louis Browns, Baltimore Orioles, the Indians, the Boston Red Sox, the Tigers again, and finally the Minnesota Twins. His lifetime average was .277 and he hit over .300 as a regular twice, in 1949 and 1950. He belted a lifetime 266 home runs.

WHAT WAS THE LARGEST NUMBER OF HOME RUNS HIT BY BOTH TEAMS IN A SEVEN GAME WORLD SERIES?

The record of 17 homers in a series was set by

the New York Yankees and Brooklyn Dodgers in 1953.

The Yankees received their power from Joe Collins (one); Billy Martin (two), who also hit .500 with a .958 slugging percentage and was named MVP of the series; Mickey Mantle, who hit two, one of them a grand slam; Gil McDougald (two); Gene Woodling and Yogi Berra (one each).

The Dodgers' power was supplied by Gil Hodges (one), Jim Gilliam (two), Billy Cox (one), Carl Furillo (one), Duke Snider (one), Roy Campanella (one), and pinch hitter George Shuba (one).

The total for both teams was 17—nine for the Yankees, eight for the Dodgers. The ERA for the Yankee staff was a whopping 4.50, while the Dodger pitchers had an equally high ERA of 4.91.

There was one exquisite pitching performance in the Series; Carl Erskine breaking Howard Ehmke's strikeout record for one game by fanning 14 in the third game. Erskine scattered six hits and the Dodgers won, 3–2, on Campanella's home run.

The rest of the pitchers had to watch their stuff get belted out of the park in this record home-run battle. The main reason for the carnage was that the both clubs were slugger-filled: the Dodgers hit 139 that season, the Yanks 208, to lead the league.

WHO WAS THE ONLY NEW YORK YANKEE TO HIT A HOME RUN IN HIS FIRST AT BAT IN THE MAJOR LEAGUES?

Ironically, it was not a well-known Yankee slugger of the Mickey Mantle genre, but rather, a chap named Johnny Miller, who did it on September 11, 1966. Miller played only six games for the Bronx

Bombers, batting .087, before departing for the minors. He made another big-league appearance in 1969 with the Los Angeles Dodgers, for whom he played 26 games and batted .211. He hit exactly two home runs in his entire major league career.

HOW MANY 20-GAME WINNERS DID THE MIGHTY 1927 YANKEES HAVE?

One and only one.

The 1927 Yankees, one of the most fearsome teams the game has known, relied heavily on their bats. Lou Gehrig hit .373, with 175 runs batted in and 47 home runs. Tony Lazzeri stole 22 bases and hit .309, while slamming 18 home runs. Babe Ruth smote a then-record 60 home runs, drove in 164 runs, and finished with a whopping .356 batting average. Earle Combs enjoyed a .356 average and a league-leading total of 23 triples. Bob Meusel stole 24 bases, hit .337, and knocked in 103 runs. The team's combined batting average was .307.

But the only 20-game winner was Waite Hoyt. Hoyt won a league-leading 22 games, and lost only seven; his earned-run average was 2.64. All of the other solid Yankee pitchers—Herb Pennock, Wilcy Moore, George Pipgras, and Urban Shocker—failed to get 20 wins. Wilcy Moore, working mostly out of the bullpen, won 19 and saved 13 while leading the league in ERA (2.28). Herb Pennock came up with a 3.00 ERA and a 19–8 record. George Pipgras had a 10–3 record and a mediocre 4.12 ERA. Urban Shocker, who suffered from heart trouble all season and died two years later, still managed to win 18 and lose but six, with a 2.84 ERA. The Yankee pitchers as a unit led the league in ERA with 3.20, and won a then-record 110 games.

NAME THE FIRST BATTER TO PINCH-HIT A HOME RUN IN A WORLD SERIES?

Yogi Berra of the New York Yankees did it during the 1947 World Series against the Brooklyn Dodgers, played on October 2. In the top of the seventh, Yankee catcher Sherm Lollar, due to bat, was called back to the bench. Berra was summoned to pinch-hit. Yogi slammed a Ralph Branca fastball over the scoreboard at Ebbets Field to bring the Yankees within one run of the Dodgers, but Branca held fast and the Dodgers prevailed, 9–8.

WHO HIT THE MOST PINCH-HIT HOME RUNS IN ONE WORLD SERIES?

Chuck Essegian, a pinch-hitting outfielder for the Los Angeles Dodgers, homered twice during the 1959 World Series against the Chicago White Sox.

Essegian's first roundtripper came in the second game, played on October 2, 1959, at Comiskey Park, when in the seventh inning he batted for Johnny Podres with two away and the Sox leading, 2–1. Essegian stroked his homer off Bob Shaw, who then walked Junior Gilliam. At this juncture Charlie Neal hit his second homer of the game to put the Dodgers in front, 4–2, enabling them to win the game and tie the Series.

In the final game of the Series, Duke Snider unloaded his 11th career Series homer, in the third inning, to spark the Dodgers. In the top half of the ninth, the aging Snider was replaced by Essegian so that the speedier, defense-minded Ron Fairly could be inserted into Snider's center-field position. Essegian then tagged Ray Moore for a homer into the left-field stands, same place as before, for his record-breaker. The second homer was mere icing on an 8–3 Dodger cake.

Essegian who hit only 47 career homers, wandered around the majors as a pinch hitter before retiring with a .255 average in 404 games over five years. In 1975 Bernie Carbo, the veteran designated hitter and outfielder for the Boston Red Sox, tied Essegian's record, producing a pinch hit home run in game three and one in the dramatic game six of the 1975 World Series.

DID BABE RUTH EVER PITCH FOR THE NEW YORK YANKEES?

Yes he did, on several occasions.

In 1920 Ruth pitched one game, went four innings, and won although he gave up four runs along the way.

In 1921 he pitched twice, winning both games, although the Sultan of Swat allowed a total of ten runs and 14 hits.

In 1930 the Babe started a game and went the distance, allowing three runs and 11 hits. In 1933, he won a game, 6–5, again going the distance and this time hitting the game-winning home run to boot.

Such limited appearances did not hurt Ruth's overall earned-run average, which was a sparkling 2.24 for six years. It did help his won–loss record, which was 94–46 lifetime—a .676 winning percentage overall.

NAME THE PITCHER WHO WON THE WORLD SERIES GAME IN 1962 DURING WHICH CHUCK HILLER HIT THE FIRST NATIONAL LEAGUE SERIES GRAND SLAM (FOR THE SAN FRANCISCO GIANTS).

Don Larsen.

The former New York Yankee was pitching against his old team while wearing a San Francisco Giants uniform. Larsen was summoned in relief of Bob Bolin in the fourth game, with two on and two out in the seventh inning. Larsen walked pinch hitter Yogi Berra and induced Tony Kubek to ground out to end the rally.

Larsen was scheduled to bat in the bottom of the seventh inning, but the Giants pinch-hit with Ed Bailey. The Yanks called on reliever Marshall Bridges, and in no time at all the Giants had loaded the bases. Chuck Hiller then hit his record shot, putting the Giants in front to stay. Don Larsen chalked up a Series win by officially facing only one batter. The victory came on the sixth anniversary of his perfect game against the Brooklyn Dodgers.

Larsen pitched for a number of teams from 1953 to 1967, with varying degrees of success. His lifetime earned-run average was 3.78. Overall, he lost 91 and won 81. In 1954 he was a 20-game loser. In 1956 he enjoyed his best year, winning 11 and losing five, as well as hurling the perfect game in the Series. Good with the bat, he was occasionally used as a pinch hitter and at times would bat seventh and play the outfield. He retired with a .242 average as a hitter—exceptionally good for a pitcher.

WHO HIT THE SECOND NATIONAL LEAGUE WORLD SERIES GRAND SLAM?

Chuck Hiller hit the first World Series slam for the San Francisco Giants in 1962, and the second was hit two years later by Ken Boyer of the St. Louis Cardinals, on October 11, 1964, in game four of the St. Louis-Yankees Series. The Yankees were ahead, two games to one, at the time, and were leading in the fourth game, 3–0, in the top of the sixth inning. Cardinal starter Ray Sadecki had been knocked out in the first, and now reliever Roger Craig was pitching.

In the top of the sixth St. Louis loaded the bases. Ken Boyer, the Cardinal third baseman, now stepped to the plate; that season Boyer hit .295 and had 24 home runs and 119 runs batted in to lead the National League. He ripped the pitch from Al Downing to right field and the bleachers therein, to put the Cards out in front, 4–3. (Downing later was also the victim of Hank Aaron's record-breaking 715th homer).

The homer tied the series at two games apiece, and the Cards went on to win it in seven.

HOW MANY PITCHES DID NEW YORK YANKEES' RIGHTY DON LARSEN THROW IN HIS PERFECT GAME IN THE 1956 WORLD SERIES?

It took Don Larsen 97 pitches to dispose of one of the most formidable batting orders in the majors, the 1956 Brooklyn Dodgers, on October 8, 1956.

The game, which took place in Yankee Stadium, was the high point in Larsen's career. His foe was Sal Maglie, nicknamed the Barber, who didn't have a bad day himself, giving up only five hits and two runs, one of them a Mickey Mantle homer. Maglie was good, but Larsen was better.

That year, Larsen was 11–5 with a 3.25 earned-run average.

CAN YOU RECALL EITHER OF THE TWO BIG LEAGUE TEAMS KNOWN AS THE HIT-LESS WONDERS?

Both the 1906 Chicago White Sox and the 1965 Los Angeles Dodgers were labeled Hitless Wonders, since they both won the pennant with very low team batting averages.

The 1906 White Sox, who had a team batting average of .230, depended on great pitching. They had Nick Altrock, who won 20, lost 13, and compiled a 2.06 earned-run average. There was also Big Ed Walsh, who pitched ten shutouts to lead the American League, while going 17–13 with 271 strikeouts and a superb 1.88 ERA. The Sox staff was rounded out by Doc White, who led the league in ERA with 1.52 and won 18 while losing six. Finally, Frank Owen won 22 and lost only 13 with a 2.33 ERA. The team ERA was 2.13.

The Pale Hose had no .300-hitting regulars but did have four players with more than 25 stolen bases. Their best hitter was second baseman Frank Isbell, who hit .279.

The other Hitless Wonders, the 1965 Dodgers, did have on their roster one batter who could hit with great power and average, Tommy Davis—but Davis was sidelined for almost the entire season with an ankle injury. The Dodgers hit only 78 homers, worst in the league, and had no .300 hitters among the regulars. The Dodgers' best hitter was Maury Wills, who hit .286 and stole a league-leading 94 bases. Their main offensive weapon was the stolen base, and they could live on one or two runs.

The balance wheel was Sandy Koufax, who struck out 382, won 26 and lost only eight for a league-leading .765 winning percentage, and chalked up a 2.04 ERA. Koufax started every fourth day, as did Claude Osteen who had a 15–15 record and a 2.79 ERA, with 162 strikeouts. Don Drysdale won 23, lost 12, and fanned 210. Finally, when the going got tough, the Dodgers called upon crack reliever Ron Perranoski to save the game, which he did 17 times, thanks to a 2.23 ERA.

Both the Dodgers and the White Sox won their respective pennants and went on to win the World Series, in both cases defeating hard-hitting clubs by using splendid pitching and speed on the basepaths.

NAME THE BALLPLAYER WHO ONCE WAS A VENDOR IN THE STADIUM HE WOULD PLAY IN AS A BIG LEAGUER.

Eddie Glynn of the 1980 New York Mets worked as a vendor in Shea Stadium when he was a teenager.

The reliever lived less than two miles from Shea when the ball park opened in 1964. Eddie became a vendor in 1967.

Glynn recalled, "I wasn't into the vendor tricks, like tossing peanuts and catching coins." He was more intent on studying the styles of the various players. In 1972 Glynn signed with the Detroit Tiger organization. He was traded in 1979 to the Mets for pitcher Mardie Cornejo.

Upon his return to Shea, Glynn remarked, "It was like a dream come true. I'd go around talking to the vendors and fans after a game. But it worked the other way, too. If I had a bad game, the fans would get on me. 'Hey, Glynn, go back to selling hot dogs.'"

In May 1980, the Mets held a Hot Dog day and gave Glynn a hot dog vending tray with his number, 48, embossed on the side. Glynn responded by climbing into the stands and hawking hot dogs.

WHAT WAS THE ONLY TEAM IN HISTORY TO HAVE THREE MEN WHO HIT OVER 40 HOME RUNS IN THE SAME YEAR?

The 1973 Atlanta Braves roster included Dave Johnson, the second baseman, who hit 43 home runs; Darrell Evans, with 41; and Henry Aaron, with 40. The power of Evans and Aaron had been evident before, but Johnson was a surprise: apart from that one year, he never hit more than 18 homers in a season in his career as a second baseman with the Orioles, Braves, Phillies, and Cubs.

Johnson's success with the Braves was at least partially attributable to the dimensions of Atlanta's Veteran's Stadium, a small park conducive to home runs. Playing an entire year in that ball park aided Johnson's cause. His 43 home runs turned out to be an all-time record for a second-baseman. The trio of Aaron, Evans and Johnson totaled 124 roundtrippers.

Ironically, the bats of Evans, Aaron, and Johnson could not save the Braves, who finished fifth, barely ahead of the last-place San Diego Padres, in the Western Division of the National League.

CAN YOU NAME ANY OF THE FRAN-
CHISES IN THE NATIONAL LEAGUE AT THE
TIME IT WAS ORGANIZED IN 1876?

The year the National League went into business
it boasted eight clubs, a number it preserved until
the expansion of 1962. The teams were the Philadelphia Athletics, owned by Thomas Smith and managed by Harry Wright; the Boston Red Stockings,
under Nathaniel Apollonio and Harry Wright; the
Chicago White Stockings, under William Hulbert and
Al Spalding; the Hartford Dark Blues, under Morgan
Bulkeley and Robert Ferguson; the Louisville Grays,
led by Walter Haldeman and John Chapman; the
New York Mutuals, under William Cammeyer, who
was both manager and owner; and finally, the St.
Louis Brown Stockings, under John Lucas and S.
Mason Graffen.

Of these clubs, the Mutuals eventually became
the Brooklyn Dodgers, the Athletics ultimately moved
to the American League, the Red Stockings and the
Brown Stockings also switched, and the White Stockings became the Chicago Cubs. The Hartford Dark
Blues moved to New York to become the Giants, and
the Louisville Grays switched to Pittsburgh and became the Pirates.

HOW DID A BATTING CHAMPION SUC-
CESSFULLY CONVINCE A TEAMMATE THAT
THE WORLD WAS FLAT?

James "Deacon" White of the Boston Red Stockings was the National League's batting champion in
1877.

In an era when smoking and drinking was commonplace among ball players, White neither smoked nor drank, but nurtured one idiosyncrasy: he implicitly believed that the world was flat. White was serious about his theory and spent considerable time trying to convince others, especially fellow teammates.

Naturally, White was frequently ridiculed, but one year Boston shortstop Jack Rowe came to him with a willingness to be convinced. White began asking Rowe how trees, buildings, animals, and human beings could remain on the earth if it was spinning around. He then concluded his argument by asking how a fly ball hit high in the air could possibly come back into his hands if the earth were moving. That was enough for Rowe, who became the team's only other flat-earther.

HOW DID A .400 BATTER HAVE HIS OFFICIAL BATTING AVERAGE REDUCED TO .317?

Cap Anson, the first major leaguer to get 3,000 hits, was credited in 1879 with a .407 average on 90 hits in 221 at-bats for the White Stockings of Chicago. A check of published daily box scores by the National League officials, however, revealed that he apparently had had only 72 hits in 227 trips to the plate, for a .317 figure.

Soon it was discovered that the league secretary, Nick Young, occasionally added a few hits to his favorites' totals when he compiled the official statistics. Published averages at that time were prone to error, so Young could get away with slight skulduggery. Another time, Young credited 57 stolen bases to a player named Bug Holliday, who that year (1896) stole only one base for the Cincinnati Reds, according to the records at Baseball's Hall of Fame.

Anson is now credited by the Hall of Fame with 90 hits in 227 at bats during the 1879 campaign, an average of .396.

WHICH NOTED PITCHER BECAME HENRY AARON'S MOST FREQUENT HOME RUN VICTIM?

Henry Aaron sent Don Drysdale to the bridge more often than any other pitcher he faced. Drysdale gave up 17 home runs to Aaron.

Drysdale, who spent his entire major league career with the Dodgers, also held the record for most consecutive scoreless innings pitched—58⅔ in 1968, the so-called Year of the Pitcher.

Aaron's other top victims were

Claude Osteen, Dodgers	(13)
Bob Friend, Pirates	(13)
Roger Craig, various	(10)
Don Cardwell, Cards	(10)
Larry Jackson, Cards	(10)
Vernon Law, Phillies	(9)
Robin Roberts, Phillies	(9)

WHEN HENRY AARON BROKE BABE RUTH'S RECORD OF 714 CAREER HOME RUNS, HE PLAYED RIGHT FIELD AND MISSED A CONSIDERABLE NUMBER OF GAMES. WHO WAS THE REGULAR RIGHT FIELDER FOR THE ATLANTA BRAVES?

Henry Aaron is not even listed in the *Baseball Encyclopedia* as a regular outfielder for the Atlanta Braves in 1974, since he only played in 89 games.

Dusty Baker was the regular right fielder. The regular outfielders comprised the strong-armed trio of Baker, Ralph Garr, and Rowland Office. Baker was a strongman who hit 20 home runs and batted .256. Office played center, which was dubbed Rowland's Office by the Braves. He had a good defensive year but was poor offensively, with a .246 average. Left fielder Ralph Garr collected 214 hits, and his 17 triples and .353 average led the league in those departments.

The Braves had a superior outfield with strong hitting and solid defense, but the regular outfielders' efforts went unnoticed because of Hank Aaron and his record-breaking bat.

CAN YOU RECALL WHO WAS RESPONSI- BLE FOR THE SINGLE GREATEST INNING FOR RUNS SCORED IN THE POST-1900 ERA?

On June 18, 1953, the Boston Red Sox broke a previously close game wide open by scoring 17 runs in the seventh inning against the Detroit Tigers.

No less than 23 Red Sox batters came to the plate, collecting 11 singles, two doubles, a home run (by Dick Gernert), and six walks. The principal victim of this carnage was Steve Gromek, a pitcher who had just been acquired from the Cleveland Indians. Gromek recalled, "They got some clean hits, but most of them were flukes. The ball kept bouncing just out of reach of our infielders or falling in front of our outfielders. I never saw anything like it."

Tiger manager Fred Hutchinson lifted Gromek after he had allowed nine earned runs. For minutes on end Gromek sat in front of his locker, seemingly in a state of shock. "I was wondering if that was the end, if I was to keep right on going to the minors. I was feeling pretty sick."

Ultimately the Red Sox won the game, 23–3. Gene Stephens got three hits in the seventh inning, which lasted 48 minutes. The only good news for the Tigers was that only 3,198 people saw the game at Fenway Park.

Following his debacle, Gromek came to the ball park every day for five days until manager Hutchinson said his first words to him, "Gromek, you pitch today," against the Athletics. Gromek, his morale restored, promptly pitched a five-hit shutout against the hapless A's.

IN 1959, LOS ANGELES BASEBALL FANS HONORED A MAN THEY NEVER SAW PLAY FOR OR AGAINST THE CALIFORNIA TEAM. WHO WAS THE PLAYER?

Roy Campanella, the Brooklyn Dodgers' All-Star catcher was tragically paralyzed following an automobile accident in January 1958, while still a member of the Dodgers. He was totally immobile, utterly dependent on others. Throughout 1958, Campanella was secluded in his hospital room, visible only to his wife and doctors. In 1959, following extensive rehabilitation, Campy was released from the hospital, although permanently confined to a wheelchair.

On May 7, 1959, the New York Yankees and the Los Angeles Dodgers played an exhibition game in

77

honor of Roy. Before the game started, he was wheeled in to the Los Angeles Coliseum by friend and shortstop Pee Wee Reese. He made a speech from second base to the 93,103 fans in attendance.

Between the fifth and sixth innings, the Coliseum's lights were cut, and announcer John Ramsey asked everyone in the stadium to rise, holding a lighted match or cigarette lighter in tribute to Roy. Vince Scully, the Dodgers' announcer, called the demonstration "Ninety-three thousand prayers for a great man."

DURING A MAJOR-LEAGUE GAME IN 1959, TWO BALLS WERE IN PLAY SIMULTANEOUSLY. HOW DID THAT HAPPEN?

Two balls in play? Yes indeed. The oddity happened on June 30, 1959, during a game between the Chicago Cubs and the St. Louis Cardinals at Wrigley Field, Chicago.

Here's how it happened. In the top of the fourth, Bob Anderson of the Cubs fired a three-and-one pitch to Stan Musial of the Cards. The pitch eluded Cubs' catcher Sammy Taylor and umpire Vic Delmore. Taylor didn't bother to go after it, believing the ball to be foul-tipped for a strike. Actually it was ball four, and Musial trotted to first. At this point, Taylor and Cubs manager Bob Scheffing rushed the umpire to argue the call. Meanwhile, the ball was still resting comfortably back at the screen.

By the time Musial arrived at first, the whole St. Louis bench pointed to the ball and urged Musial to run. Musial alertly sped for second. Realizing that the ball was still in play, third baseman Alvin Dark darted for it; Dark knew that Musial was entitled to all the bases he could get.

But before Dark could get the ball, the Cards' batboy tossed it away and it landed in the hands of Pat Pieper, the announcer at Wrigley Field. Pieper grabbed the ball and then dropped it. Meanwhile, the frantic Dark rushed up to Pieper and shouted, "Give me the ball!"

"I haven't got it," said Pieper. "There it is"— pointing at the ground. Dark grabbed the ball and whipped it to shortstop Ernie Banks at second base. Suddenly, a second ball whizzed toward Banks. No, it wasn't a case of double vision. It turned out that umpire Delmore, while arguing, reached into his pocket and gave Sammy Taylor a new ball. Taylor fired it to his pitcher, Anderson, immediately. Anderson, in turn, threw the ball to Banks, but the throw was high and the ball zipped into center field. Dark's throw was low but Banks fielded it on one hop.

Musial, who successfully slid into second base, watched the Cubs' center fielder tracking down one of the two balls, so he decided to head for third. Three steps later he ran into Banks with the other ball.

Meanwhile, Bobby Thomson, the Cubs' right fielder, trapped ball number two and lobbed it casually to the Cubs' dugout. Seeing one ball in Banks' glove and another in the air, floating toward the Cubs' dugout, Musial looked disbelievingly in both directions, unable to decide what to do.

While all this was going on, Bob Scheffing, the Cubs' manager, continued arguing with the umpire Delmore. Now Solly Hemus, the Cards' manager, was on his feet, preparing a filibuster as well.

At long last the umpires decided that Musial should go back to first. Then they reversed themselves and declared Musial out. Hemus played the game under protest, but the Cards won anyway, 4–1.

WHEN GEORGE WEISS QUIT AS NEW YORK YANKEES GENERAL MANAGER IN 1960, HE MADE A PREDICTION THAT WOULD HAUNT THE BRONX BOMBERS. WHAT WAS IT?

Weiss predicted that the Yankees would crumble without him. "They [the Yankees] have five more years at the most under the new management," warned Weiss. The warning was exquisitely accurate.

After Weiss resigned, the Yankee owners spent huge sums of money to sign precious few players. After five years had passed, the Yankees comprised a relatively old and injured team, while the Bombers' farm system was barren of prospects. In time it became apparent that the roots Weiss had planted had been pulled up by his successors.

In 1965 the Yankees finished a dismal sixth, as the minor leaguers failed to produce and such stars as Roger Maris, Joe Pepitone, and Al Downing departed with age and injury. By the time George Steinbrenner bought the team in 1973, it only had six scouts.

George Weiss's prediction, ridiculed in 1960, turned out to have been frighteningly accurate.

WHO REPLACED TED WILLIAMS IN LEFT FIELD AFTER THE "SPLENDID SPLINTER" RETIRED FROM THE RED SOX?

Ted Williams played the final game of his career on September 26, 1960. Carroll Hardy, a journeyman outfielder, replaced Williams after the Splinter cracked his 521st big-league home run, in his final at bat. Hardy finished the season of 1960 in left field for the Red Sox.

The following spring the Red Sox inserted Carl Yastrzemski in left. Yaz became a Triple Crown winner in 1967 (not to mention the man with the lowest average ever to win a batting title, .301 in 1968) as well as a lifetime 3,000-hit man and 400-home-run hitter.

Actually, the Red Sox were grooming Yastrzemski as a potential replacement for Williams in the late 1950s, and the Boston brain trust was eminently insightful in this case.

WHO WAS THE FIRST SLUGGER TO HIT FOUR HOME RUNS IN TWO DIFFERENT WORLD SERIES?

The Brooklyn Dodgers' Duke Snider, who was inducted into the Hall of Fame in 1980, became the first man to swat four home runs in two World Series when he belted his second roundtripper of the fifth game of the 1955 World Series, against the Yankees. The pitcher was Bob Grim and the ball flew over the right-center field scoreboard in Ebbets Field.

Snider's first four-homer World Series came in 1952, when he hit his roundtrippers in a losing cause. His victims then were Allie Reynolds in the opener, Ewell Blackwell in the fifth game, and Vic Raschi twice in the sixth game.

In 1955 he hit one off Whitey Ford in the opener,

one off Johnny Kucks in game four, and two off Grim in game five.

Snider's lifetime home-run total in World Series play is a National League–leading 11; his lifetime mark of 407 home runs places him 18th on the all-time list. The Duke of Flatbush was elected to the Hall of Fame in 1980.

HOW LONG WAS THE SHORTEST GAME IN AMERICAN LEAGUE HISTORY?

One hour and 13 minutes.

On August 8, 1920, the Detroit Tigers, behind Howard Ehmke, beat the Yankees, 1–0. The Yankees aided the Tiger cause when outfielder Ping Bodie fell for the "hidden ball trick" with two on and none out in the fifth inning. For brevity, no other game in American League annals can match this one.

WHAT GAME-WINNING HOME RUN TURNED OUT NOT TO BE A HOME RUN AT ALL?

On April 10, 1976, at Milwaukee, the New York Yankees were leading the Brewers, 9–6, when the Brewers filled the bases in the bottom of the ninth.

Yankee ace reliever Sparky Lyle then tossed a fat pitch to Don Money and the Brewers' part-time first baseman belted it into the right-field bleachers, believing it was a grand slam home run. The Milwaukee fans went into a joyous frenzy. Meanwhile, first base umpire Bill McKean frantically consulted with his fellow umpires.

As it turned out, before the fateful pitch to Money, the Yankee manager Billy Martin, had yelled instructions to Lyle but the pitcher had not heard them. However, Chris Chambliss, the Yankee's first baseman, had heard Martin and quietly asked umpire McKean for a time-out so he could relay the word to Lyle.

McKean called for a timeout, but Lyle, still not hearing a thing, pitched to Money. Ultimately, blame for the faux pas was charged to the screaming Milwaukee fans.

Umpire McKean ordered the home run canceled. Lyle served another pitch to Money and struck him out. The Yankees eventually won, 9–7.

HOW DID THE YANKEES FARE ON MAY 2, 1939, THE FIRST TIME IN 2,130 GAMES IN WHICH THEY DID NOT HAVE LOU GEHRIG IN THE LINEUP?

On the day that Gehrig benched himself, the Yankees, playing with rookie Babe Dahlgren at first base, shellacked the Detroit Tigers, 22–2. Dahlgren hit a home run and a double to lead the Bombers' attack. Although one of their easiest wins, the game was one of the hardest to play for the Yankees.

When Gehrig emerged from the dugout at the start of the game to give the lineup card to the umpire, he was hailed with a standing ovation. The collective roar brought tears to his eyes as he walked back to the dugout.

WHO WAS KNOWN AS THE "CLOWN PRINCE OF BASEBALL"?

Al Schacht.

There are class clowns and circus clowns, and then there are baseball clowns. Schacht fell in the third category. A competent pitcher, Schacht was considered a champion clown when he first broke into the major leagues with the Washington Senators. One of his ploys was to send John McGraw a telegram every time he won a game, hoping that the New York Giants' manager would want Schacht on his team. After McGraw received the tenth message, "PITCHED SHUTOUT TODAY STOP ARM LOOSE STOP GOING STRONG," the manager replied with his own, "TIGHTEN UP DON'T STOP KEEP GOING."

When Al played in the International League, he would entertain fans between doubleheaders. One day in Baltimore, he performed with a fungo stick and a sawdust baseball called a Rocket. When the second game started, he went to the bullpen with the Rocket in his back pocket. Schacht was called on as a relief pitcher in the sixth inning with the bases loaded and nobody out—an ideal situation for the Clown Prince. He slipped the real ball inside his shirt, produced the sawdust ball, and delivered his pitch. When the batter saw the fat pitch coming, he swung hard yet got nothing but a pop-up. Easy infield out. The next batter did the same. By now Schacht's only concern was that the stitches in the Rocket would not hold. But the only thing that went flying was the opponent's bat. The ball popped up, for out number two. The third batter to face Al was Rube Parnham. Schacht once said, "I could always get him out because I'd talk to him till I got his goat and then made him swing at the bad ones." But Schacht was forced to use the sawdust ball anyway, since the real ball had squirmed to the back of his shirt. Parnham hit the ball back to Schacht, who caught it for the third out.

Now another problem confronted Schacht, who had to leave the ball on the mound before going to the dugout. Al desperately tried to get the real ball out of his shirt while he dashed for the dugout with the Rocket in his glove. But umpire Bill McGowan was on the ball—the *real* ball! He yelled to Schacht, "Throw me that ball." The lopsided Rocket had taken its last flight.

Since there was no evidence that Schacht had used the phony ball for anyone but the last batter, only the last pitch was ruled illegal. Now Parnham returned to the plate and the "real" fun began. Before each pitch, Schacht pretended that he had another sawdust ball in his jersey. He would reach into his shirt, the crowd would boo, and Parnham would ask for an examination of the ball. Naturally, the umpire would run out to the mound to investigate. Schacht constantly engaged Parnham in dialogue while this was going on. The confused batter finally missed two wide curve balls and swung wildly at a high hard one for the third strike!

One spring night in Tampa, Florida, when the Washington Senators were preparing for their season, the Clown Prince was not laughing. Bucky Harris, the team's manager, decided to play a practical joke on Schacht, for a change. Harris called Al at his hotel room and asked, "How would you like to join me on a double date? I've got a couple of nifty dames who want to play peek-a-boo at their house."

Schacht replied: "Sounds perfectly alluring. When do we start?"

"Get a bag of oranges," said Harris, "and meet me in the lobby in fifteen minutes. I've got the gin."

Schacht put on his best outfit, sprayed on some cologne, and bought a bag of oranges and a box of candy, anticipating an exotic evening to be long remembered.

Harris and Schacht then got in a cab and drove for several miles. Finally, the cab dropped them off at a beautiful residence. Bucky rang the bell. When no one came to the door, Schacht asked, "Are you sure this is the right place? It would be a helluva fix if it ain't. We're a hundred miles from nowhere and the cab is gone."

"I'm absolutely sure," replied Harris. "I was here last night."

Then the fun began. The door opened, and to Schacht's surprise, there stood a huge man holding a gun in his hand.

"So you're the so-and-sos who've been calling on my wife while I was away. I'll show you!" The man fired a shot and Harris sprawled on the steps, apparently bleeding profusely.

Schacht turned and ran. He heard a few more shots and continued to run, leaving the oranges behind. Al sprinted about a mile and then walked the rest of the 11½ miles back to Tampa, thinking of Bucky Harris. What would the Senators do without him? He worried about the potential scandal. He felt as though he could never be a clown again after what he had just gone through.

Whenever the lights of a car appeared, Schacht hid in the bushes. He didn't want to be seen or recognized near the scene of the crime. At last, one car drove past his hiding place very slowly. Schacht heard voices and uproarious laughter.

After midnight, Al finally returned to his hotel. When he turned the lights on in his room, the entire Washington team went into transports of hysterical laughter. Of course, Bucky Harris was laughing the hardest, sitting alongside an attractive woman and the huge man. Harris had red paint all over his coat and shirt.

NAME ANY OF THE PRE-1920 PLAYERS WHO "LOST" HOME RUNS BECAUSE OF THE REVERSAL OF THE "SUDDEN-DEATH HOME RUN" RULE.

As a result of the rule change, which was rendered on May 5, 1969, 37 players "lost" home runs.

Prior to the 1920 season, a team batting last that won a game in the ninth or in an extra inning by rule could not win by more than one run. If a man hit an outside-the-park home run that under present rules, could have resulted in a victory by more than one run, he was given credit for a lesser hit and only the winning run counted. At first, baseball rulemakers voted that any pre-1920 batter who hit any ball outside the park in a sudden-death situation should be given a home run. After a further review, however, that decision was reversed.

The following 37 players lost home runs because of the rulings:

DATE	BATTER	TEAM	LEAGUE	OPP.	HIT
June 17, 1884	Roger Connor	N.Y.	N.L.	Bos.	Single
Sept. 6, 1884	Hardy Richardson	Buf.	N.L.	Bos.	Triple
April 21, 1885	Fred Mann	Pitt.	A.A.	Lou.	Double
July 30, 1885	Tommy McCarthy	Bos.	N.L.	Det.	Double
Aug. 20, 1885	Paul Hines	Pro.	N.L.	Bos.	Single
June 5, 1890	Sam Thompson	Phi.	N.L.	Bkn.	Single
July 30, 1880	Al McCauley	Phi.	N.L.	Chi.	Triple
June 17, 1890	Mike Griffin	N.Y.	N.L.	Phi.	Double
May 7, 1891	King Kelly	Cin.	A.A.	Bos.	Single
Sept. 13, 1891	George Wood	Phi.	A.A.	Mil.	Double
July 7, 1892	Buck Ewing	N.Y.	N.L.	St. L.	Single
May 13, 1893	Lou Bierbauer	Pitt.	N.L.	Lou.	Single
Aug. 9, 1893	G. Van Haltren	Pitt.	N.L.	Chi.	Double
Aug. 27, 1895	Billy Lange	Chi.	N.L.	Wash.	Single
Sept. 2, 1895	Mike Tiernan	N.Y.	N.L.	Cle.	Triple
Sept. 27, 1895	Duke Farrell	N.Y.	N.L.	Bal.	Triple
July 27, 1896	Charlie Irwin	Cin.	N.L.	Cle.	Triple
June 4, 1897	Parke Wilson	N.Y.	N.L.	Lou.	Double
July 15, 1899	Jimmy Collins	Bos.	N.L.	St. L.	Single

DATE	BATTER	TEAM	LEAGUE	OPP.	HIT
July 24, 1899	Ginger Beaumont	Pitt.	N.L.	Phi.	Triple
July 24, 1900	Jimmy Collins	Bos.	N.L.	St. L.	Single
July 27, 1900	Chick Stahl	Bos.	N.L.	Pitt.	Single
May 17, 1901	Bill Coughlin	Wash.	A.L.	Phi.	Single
Sept. 1, 1902	Ed Gremminger	Bos.	N.L.	Cin.	Double
June 26, 1903	Pat Moran	Bos.	N.L.	Chi.	Triple
Sept. 10, 1904	Roger Bresnahan	N.Y.	N.L.	Phi.	Double
May 5, 1906	Sherry Magee	Phi.	N.L.	Bkn.	Triple
June 2, 1906	Tim Jordan	Bkn.	N.L.	Bos.	Double
May 25, 1908	Joe Tinker	Chi.	N.L.	N.Y.	Double
Sept. 28, 1908.	Cy Seymour	N.Y.	N.L.	Phi.	Single
April 23, 1910	Doc Crandall	N.Y.	N.L.	Bkn.	Single
April 24, 1911	Tex Erwin	Bkn.	N.L.	Chi.	Triple
June 17, 1914	Sherry Magee	Phi.	N.L.	St. L.	Double
April 19, 1917	Ping Bodie	Phi.	A.L.	Bos.	Triple
July 8, 1918	Babe Ruth	Bos.	A.L.	Cle.	Triple
July 18, 1918	Frank Baker	N.Y.	A.L.	Det.	Single
April 18, 1918	Irish Meusel	Phi.	N.L.	Bos.	Triple

DO YOU KNOW THE PLAYER WHOSE PAYCHECK WAS SENT TO HIS WIFE TO PREVENT HIM FROM SPENDING THE MONEY ON ALCOHOL?

Arthur "Bugs" Raymond. Raymond was one of the New York Giants' happy-go-lucky players during the early 1900s. After a few drinks, Bugs was capable of doing anything, and usually did. He would disappear for days to escape Manager John McGraw's wrath.

McGraw, in turn, would mail Raymond's salary directly to Mrs. Raymond with instructions not to let Bugs have a penny of it—but Raymond once found a way. Instead of warming up in the bullpen, he swapped the ball for as many drinks as the market would bring. Then he disappeared for four days.

One afternoon McGraw told Raymond what he thought of a man who would leave his team during a hard pennant fight. At that Bugs responded, "Since yer payin' 'er, let me wife pitch fer de pennant."

Bugs had made his point. McGraw made a new deal and Raymond was given his check along with a personal guard, who was instructed to buy him root beer, lemonade, and sarsaparilla whenever he was thirsty.

The crafty Bugs, however, still managed to get more than just a soft drink. So once again, Raymond's paycheck was taken away from him and he was put on a moderate allowance of spending money. Bugs got around that by going into saloons where he was known and saying to the patrons, "Lissen, ya lugs, I got just one dollar to buy drinks tonight; so I'm standin' a round of beer, and youse guys are buyin' me whiskey." That provided Raymond with 19 whiskeys for one glass of beer, which to him was a fair arrangement.

WHEN WAS THE FIRST NATIONAL LEAGUE GAME PLAYED? NAME THE TEAMS, THE PLAYERS WHO PARTICIPATED, AND THE RECORDS SET IN THAT GAME THAT NEVER WILL BE BROKEN.

The first National League game ever played took place in Philadelphia on Saturday, April 22, 1876. The two teams involved were the Athletics and Boston Red Stockings. Boston won, 6–5, before 3,000 onlookers.

Since this was the only organized baseball played that day, a number of "firsts" took place that will remain forever etched in the record books. To wit:

• The first National League player to go to bat was George Wright, shortstop and leadoff man for the Red Stockings. Wright grounded to short, and within three seconds Davy Force had the first National League assist and Wes Fisler, the Athletics' first baseman, the first putout.

• Andy Leonard was then retired, but Jim O'Rourke, the center fielder and third Boston batter, delivered the first National League hit, a single to left.

• Tim McGinley, the Boston catcher, who batted sixth, scored the first National League run in the second inning. He crossed the plate after George Hall, the Athletics' left fielder, caught a long fly off the bat of Jack Manning, who thus was responsible for the first run batted in, although scorers of the day did not keep track of RBIs.

• The Athletics produced some firsts of their own. In the home half of the first inning, Levi

Meyerle, the second baseman, smashed the league's first double. (Two days later, in the same park, Meyerle hit the first triple.) But the initial home run was not struck until May 2, when, in the fifth inning of a game at Cincinnati, Ross Barnes of Chicago connected with a pitch by William "Cherokee" Fisher and crashed it deep into the outfield grass.

WHO HAD THE LONGEST STREAK OF NO-HIT BALL?

Johnny Vander Meer of the Cincinnati Reds pitched 21⅓ innings of consecutive no-hit ball on June 11 and 15, 1938.

In 1938 Bill McKechnie was hired as the manager of the Reds. McKechnie changed Vander Meer's delivery and helped him cut down on his wildness, which had caused him to fail earlier in his career with the Boston and Brooklyn organizations. Johnny's new windup (a rocking-chair delivery) paid off on June 11, when he stopped the Boston Braves at Cincinnati, 3–0, without allowing a single hit.

The first night game at Ebbets Field, Brooklyn, turned out to be the backdrop for Vander Meer's second no-hitter. On the night of June 15, 1938, the noisy Brooklyn crowd, hostile to Vandy as the game began, was stunned into silence as he kept mowing down the hometown hitters. Soon the partisan rooters began to cheer the enemy pitcher.

But with one out in the last half of the ninth and the Reds leading by 6–0, Vander Meer experienced a sudden streak of wildness. He walked Babe Phelps, Cookie Lavagetto, and Dolf Camilli of the Dodgers on only 18 pitches. Manager McKechnie strolled out to the mound to relax him. When play resumed, Ernie Koy of the Dodgers smashed the ball to Lew Riggs at third. Riggs threw to the plate to force Goody Rosen, who was running for Phelps. Leo Durocher then popped to short center, and when Harry Craft came in to make the catch, the no-hitter was preserved and history made. Vander Meer allowed a hit on June 19, 1938 at Boston, a third-inning single by Debs Garms.

WHAT MAJOR-LEAGUE MANAGER CREATED HIS OWN "BONEHEAD CLUB"?

The Bonehead Club was the brainstorm of zany manager "Uncle" Wilbert Robinson, of the Brooklyn Dodgers.

In starting this unusual club Robinson originally hoped to cure his team of its habit of committing bonehead plays. "It ain't fair to the guys who are hustling to lose on account of the boners that some other guys pull," said Robinson. "From now on whenever anyone makes a dumb play, he's got to kick in 10 bucks to the club treasury. At the end of the year, all the players will split the money. And if you keep on the way you've been going, you'll get more money out of it than the winners of the World Series."

The players agreed, but it was the manager who became a charter member of the Bonehead Club—that same afternoon he handed the umpire his laundry list instead of the batting order.

One of Uncle Robbie's problems was that he had difficulty remembering his players names. On successive days, one player, Jimmy Johnston, was put in the starting lineup at first base, second, shortstop, and third; then back around at left, center and right field.

Another time, he planned putting Oscar Roettger in right field. "How do you spell Oscar's last name?" he asked the player sitting next to him on the bench. The player didn't know, either. "To hell with it," said Robbie and he put down *C-O-X*. So Dick Cox played right field that day.

Some sportswriters criticized Robbie's illogical method of picking a lineup. So, during one losing streak, Robbie made them a proposal: "Yuh second guessers are always winning the games in your columns. Why don't yuh pick me a team that'll win out there on the field?"

The writers took him up on the challenge. Each one made out a batting order. Robbie picked one from the pile and handed it to the umpire. That particular lineup put Babe Herman, whom Robinson was then using at first base, in left field. Other than that there were no major changes.

The Dodgers led the St. Louis Cardinals by a run heading into the ninth inning. But in the top of the ninth Rogers Hornsby came to bat with two men on base and two out. He hit a long fly to left. Herman chased it, overran the ball, then, trying to save the situation, got himself bumped on the head with the ball. All the baserunners scored and the Cards won the game.

Robbie dashed into the press box, yelling, "Who's the ignorant dummy that put the Babe in left field?"

A PLAYER'S FAILURE TO TOUCH SECOND BASE DURING THE 1908 PENNANT RACE COST THE NEW YORK GIANTS THE CHAMPIONSHIP. WHO WAS THE CULPRIT?

Fred Merkle.

The episode took place on September 23, 1908, at the Polo Grounds in Manhattan. Merkle was a 19-year-old first baseman appearing in his first full National League game. The Giants at the time held first place by six percentage points over their opponents that afternoon, the Chicago Cubs.

With the score tied, 1–1, and two out in the last half of the ninth inning, Moose McCormick of the Giants was on third and Merkle on first. When Al Bridwell singled to center field and McCormick crossed the plate with what appeared to be the winning run, the jubilant crowd surged on to the field. But Merkle, seeing McCormick score, had never bothered to continue to second base. Instead, he ran to the clubhouse to escape the onrushing fans. Meanwhile, Solly Hoffman, the Cubs' center fielder, threw the ball toward second base, but his throw was wild. Floyd Kroh, a substitute, attempted to retrieve it, but Joe McGinnity raced over from the Giants' coaching box, wrestled him for it, and is believed to have thrown it into the stands. Somehow the second baseman obtained another ball, stepped on second, and raced over to the plate umpire, Hank O'Day. The first-base umpire, Robert Emslie, had been watching first and missed the play entirely. But when O'Day told him what had happened, Emslie called Merkle out.

O'Day, an umpire in the league as early as 1888, went back to his hotel and after eating dinner, sat down and wrote the following letter to Harry C. Pulliam, president of the National League:

HARRY C. PULLIAM, ESQ.
            PRES. NAT. LEAGUE

Dear Sir:

In the Game today at New York between New York and Chicago, in the last half of the ninth inning the score was tied 1–1. New York was at the bat, with two men out, McCormick of New York on 3rd base and Merkle of N.Y. on 1st base; Bridwell was at bat and hit a clean single Base-Hit to center field. Merkle did not run the ball out; he started toward second base, but on getting half way there he turned and ran down the field toward the club house. The ball was fielded in to second base for a Chicago man to make the play, when McGinnity ran from the coacher's box out in the field to second base and interfered with the play being made. Emslie, who said he did not watch Merkle, asked if Merkle touched second base. I said he did not. Then Emslie called Merkle out, and I would not allow McCormick's run to score. The game at the end of the ninth inning was 1–1. The people ran out on the field. I did not ask to have the field cleared, as it was too dark to continue play.

Your Respt,

                              Henry O'Day

To understand properly the meaning of the Merkle play and to determine whether O'Day and Emslie made a good decision, some background is necessary. The rules, of course, are quite clear that when the third out of an inning is a force-out, no runs can score on the play. The trouble was, the rule had never been enforced.

Less than three weeks earlier, on September 4, in a game between Pittsburgh and Chicago, a Pirate runner, Warren Gill, did exactly what Merkle did.

O'Day was umpiring that game and refused to call Gill out. He couldn't confer with anyone, as he was umpiring the game alone. But after thinking about it, O'Day determined that if the play ever happened again, he would call the runner out.

So there never would have been a Merkle story if O'Day had not been the umpire behind the plate, or if the play on Gill had not come up, or if the same man, Bud Evers, had not been playing second base. It was an unusual and coincidental set of circumstances.

Bill Klem, one of the best known of all major-league umpires, always insisted that the decision on Merkle was the worst in the history of baseball. Klem's thinking was that the rule in question was intended to apply only to infield grounders and not to safe hits. However, O'Day interpreted the rule as written.

Both the Giants and the Cubs protested the decision of the umpires to replay the "tied" game. The Giants claimed that they had legitimately won the game, 2–1. The Cubs maintained that they should be awarded the game by forfeit, first because of McGinnity's interference and then because the Giants had refused to play the game the following day, as required by league rules.

Despite Pulliam's decision to side with the umpires, the two teams continued their protest to the league's board of directors, which ordered the game replayed on October 8.

The Giants and Cubs were tied for first place on the day of the replayed game, each with 98–55 records. The Cubs defeated the Giants, 4–2, and annexed the championship.

In failing to touch second base, Merkle only did what many players had already done, yet he was called every epithet printable and some that weren't. *The Sporting Life,* a baseball publication, noted that "through the inexcusable stupidity of Merkle, a substitute, the Giants had a sure victory turned into a doubtful one, a game was played in dispute, a complicated and disagreeable controversy was started, and perhaps the championship imperilled or lost."

Apparently, the only prominent sportswriter to take a sensible view of the affair was Paul W. Eaton, a freelance writer in Washington, D.C. "A protest may well be recorded against the many severe criticisms of Merkle that have been made." Eaton wrote. "His accusers seem to have agreed on the epithet of 'bonehead.' It can be stated most emphatically that in failing to touch second after Bridwell's hit, Merkle did only what had been done in hundreds of championship games in the major leagues."

Merkle, understandably heartbroken, returned to his parents' home in Toledo, Ohio. Reporters crowded around him there, swarming like bees. Merkle then told a side of the story that had eluded everyone—that his hit that sent McCormick to third might easily have been for extra bases.

"The single that set up the play might have been a double or a triple," he explained. "But Jack Hayden, the Cub right fielder, made a wonderful stab and knocked down the drive. At that I could have gone to second easily, but with one run needed to win and a man on third, I played it safe. When Bridwell got the single that should have won the game, I was so happy over the victory I started for the clubhouse, figuring, of course, on getting out of the way before the crowd blocked the field. When I heard Evers calling for the ball, and noticed the excitement, I did not know at first what it was about, but the meaning of it all suddenly dawned on me and I wished that a large, roomy and comfortable hole would open up and swallow me. But it is all over now and will have to be forgotten."

But seven years later, the play was not forgotten. At that time a writer asked Merkle, "Do you get any fun out of baseball?"

"No," Merkle replied, "I wouldn't call it fun. I have a too rough a time out there."

"Do the fans still ride you?"

"Yes. The worst thing is, I can't do things other players do without attracting attention. Little slips that would be excused in other players are burned into me by the crowds. Of course, I have made mistakes with the rest, but I have to do double duty. If any play I'm concerned with goes wrong, I'm the fellow who gets the blame, no matter where the thing went off the line. I try not to mind it too much; I've been ridden enough to get used to it, but nobody's as thick-skinned but what a roast will get under his skin at some time or another."

The Merkle play was such a "touching" story that the following year a book called *Touching Second* was written for the second baseman, Evers, by Hughie Fullerton.

Surprisingly, there is reason to believe that Merkle did touch second. But not exactly right after the incident. Tom Meany, a baseball authority and author, once learned that after the game, Merkle's manager saw to it that Merkle was secluded in the Shelbourne Hotel in Brighton Beach, Brooklyn, and that in the middle of the night he had the boy return to the Polo Grounds and touch second, so that if he were ever asked under oath he could swear that on September 23, 1908, he had touched second!

WHAT HALL OF FAMER COULD SPEND MONEY FASTER THAN HE COULD HIT HOME RUNS (WHICH HE ALSO DID VERY WELL)?

George Herman "Babe" Ruth.

Ruth once was presented with a check for $25,000 after making a movie in Cuba. He carried the check in his wallet along with his small bills until it became a frazzled piece of wastepaper.

Another time, Ruth played a five-week vaudeville engagement in Chicago, for which he was paid another $25,000. When he arrived at his hotel suite, the Babe ordered the closets filled with bottles of wine and whiskey at the cost of $3,000. He told the bootlegger to keep the closets filled with booze throughout his stay. By the end of the engagement, Ruth had spent $30,000. When a friend said to the Babe that that was no way to make money, Ruth replied, "Yeah, I found that out!"

Fortunately for Ruth, he was well paid by the Yankees. In one salary dispute during the Great Depression, Yankee owner Colonel Jacob Ruppert, who talked with a heavy German accent, said to Ruth, "You vant more money? You now have a bigger salary dan President Hoofer."

"That's right," said the Babe. "From what I hear, Hoover don't bat as high in the Presidents' League as I do in mine."

But what many people forget about Ruth, the Sultan of Swat, is that he didn't only have a high batting average, but a low earned-run average, too.

Before he became a full-time hitter, he was a superb pitcher. His record of 29⅔ consecutive scoreless innings of World Series' pitching stood for nearly 50 years, until Whitey Ford broke it.

His hitting speaks for itself: 60 home runs in one season, 714 career homers.

In one game Ruth called his shot, pointing to a spot in distant center field where he intended to deposit the ball. He then hit Charley Root's next pitch there for a homer. That was in the 1932 World Series, at Chicago. Nine years earlier, Babe's Yankees had faced the favored New York Giants in the World Series. John McGraw, who managed the Giants, refused to heed advice about pitching carefully to the Babe. "Why shouldn't we pitch to Ruth?" snapped McGraw. "I've said before and I'll say again, we pitch to better hitters than Ruth in the National League." That day Ruth went out and simply won the game with two home runs.

One manager thought he found the secret to stopping Ruth. He told his rookie pitcher, "When you pitch to the Babe, get your strikes in right at the knees and on the inside corner of the plate." On his first at bat, Ruth smacked one such "secret" pitch to right field for a double; the second time up, Ruth shifted his feet a bit and drilled the low inside pitch to left field for another double. When Ruth arrived for his third try, the rookie threw three straight balls, all too low and inside. Then he grooved a fastball down the middle and Ruth clobbered the ball into the center-field bleachers.

The manager yanked his pitcher off the mound. "Didn't I tell you to throw them at the knees?" he questioned.

"Yes sir."

"Well, why the hell didn't you follow instructions?"

"I tried, sir," replied the rookie, "but he can hit those pitches a helluva lot easier than I can throw them!"

WHO WAS THE FIRST MAJOR LEAGUE PLAYER TO ENTER THE ARMED FORCES IN THE WORLD WAR II ERA?

Eugene Stackowiack.

A rookie pitcher with the Chicago White Sox (he called himself "Gene Stack"), Stackowiack entered the army in January 1941. He died of heart trouble on June 27, 1942, after pitching for an army team at Michigan City, Indiana. The first major-league regular to enter the service was Hugh Mulcahy, a first-rate pitcher for the Philadelphia Phillies. Mulcahy, drafted on March 8, 1941, missed almost five full seasons at the peak of his career. He didn't return to the Phillies until the last days of the 1945 season.

By the time the 1942 season opened, more than 100 National League players were in the armed forces. Some club owners believed that major league baseball might be suspended for the duration of the war, but President Franklin Delano Roosevelt delivered his famed "green light" letter of January 15, 1942, in which he asserted, "I honestly think it would be best for the country to keep baseball going."

WHICH "WAR" WAS THE MOST DESTRUC-
TIVE TO ORGANIZED BASEBALL?

The Brotherhood War of 1885 was one of the most turbulent upheavals in baseball history. It resulted in the impoverishment of several club owners, the death of the American Association, a decline in attendance, and almost the destruction of the National League.

The Brotherhood was organized in 1885 as a benevolent and protective organization for the players. Its founder, Billy Voltz, was a baseball writer as well as the manager of various minor-league teams. Every player was asked to contribute five dollars each month to a fund that would be available to ill players or indigent players. When 200 players enrolled that year, a pool of $6,000 became available to the needy.

The Brotherhood took on a more formal tone at a meeting on October 22, 1885, organized by members of the National League's New York team. They signed the following preamble:

> We, the undersigned professional baseball players, recognizing the importance of united effort and impressed with the necessity in our behalf, do form ourselves this day into an organization to be known as the "Brotherhood of Professional Baseball Players." The objects we seek to accomplish are:
>
> To protect and benefit ourselves collectively and individually.
>
> To promote a high standard of professional conduct.
>
> To foster and encourage the interests of the game of baseball.

The members selected John Montgomery Ward as president and Tim Keefe as secretary. The other original members of the organization included Joe

Gerhardt, Buck Ewing, Roger Connor, Danny Richardson, Mickey Welch, Mike Dorgan, and Jim O'Rourke.

During the 1886 season, Ward began to organize chapters in other National League cities. The first to join was Detroit, which soon was followed by Chicago, Kansas City, Boston, Philadelphia, and Washington. By this time most of the prominent players in the league had entered the ranks.

Although the Brotherhood was not designed to fight club owners, most meetings consisted of little more than a debate on antimanagement grievances, of which there were many.

What the players initially demanded was recognition. Ward, Ned Hanlon, and Dan Brothers formed a committee and attended the National League meeting in 1887. A former player, Al Spalding, convinced his fellow baseball magnates that they should listen to the complaints. When an objection was made to the reserve caluse, Ward's committee was told to devise a better system of running the game. Ward admitted that this could not be done, and the case was closed.

A year later, Spalding organized baseball's first world tour. He took his Chicago team and an all-star club of National League opponents on a journey that began in Chicago on October 20, 1888, and included stops for exhibition games at San Francisco, Honolulu, Sydney, Melbourne, Colombo, Cairo, Naples, Rome, Paris, London, and many other cities.

The teams returned to New York just before the opening of the 1889 season, ending the tour with a mammoth banquet at Delmonico's Restaurant, at which A.G. Mills presided and which was attended by such celebrities as Mark Twain and Theodore

Roosevelt. Here, the players learned that during their absence, John T. Brush, a new power in the league and president of the Indianapolis team, had managed to secure approval of an absurd salary-classification plan. The players of the league were to be graded into classes from A to E, with salaries that ranged from $1,500 to $2,500.

The players realized that they were helpless to do anything about it before the 1889 season began. They insisted on an immediate hearing, but the league refused, and Ward, who had been one of the Spalding tourists, suggested a stronger response.

"There remained nothing else for the players to do but begin organizing on a new basis," said Ward.

A meeting was held of the various Brotherhood chapters' representatives at the Fifth Avenue Hotel in New York on July 14, 1889. Each representative was instructed to find the necessary capital in his own city and to report back at an early date. The reports were all encouraging. Men were found willing to advance the necessary funds to launch a new league upon terms more liberal to the players. Many of them were even willing to put in capital without any return whatever, out of sheer love for the sport.

The players announced their intention of withdrawing from the National League on November 6, 1889, and although little more than five months remained before the new season was to begin, the Brotherhood was able to build parks in eight cities and field sufficient teams for the 1890 campaign. The league, which came to be called both the Brotherhood League and the Players League, included teams from Boston, Brooklyn, New York, Chicago, Philadelphia, Pittsburgh, Cleveland, and Buffalo.

The warring leagues adopted conflicting schedules, lied about their attendance, spread false rumors, and battled for patronage. The real-estate operators and utility magnates who had backed the Brotherhood League soon lost their early enthusiasm. Meanwhile, the National League owners, beset by poor attendance, suffered even more.

The one National League owner the players least wanted to hurt, John B. Day of the New York Giants, was ruined for life. The Brotherhood players begged him to come to the outlaw league with them, but he remained loyal to the National League. Loans kept him afloat for a while, but he finally surrendered his franchise to new ownership. For a time Day managed the Giants on the field for a nominal salary, then he became an inspector of players and umpires and eventually a pensioner. Day had been offered $25,000 a year and 50 percent of the New York team's stock, to act as president of the Brotherhood.

After the 1890 season, the Brotherhood beseeched the National League for a truce. Spalding informed the players that his terms were unconditional surrender. To his astonishment, the players, unaware that the National League also was suffering terribles losses, immediately agreed, and the war was over.

IN THE EARLY DAYS OF PROFESSIONAL BASEBALL, A PINCH HITTER WAS FRIGHTENED AWAY FROM HOME PLATE BY AN UMPIRE. WHO WAS THE BALL PLAYER?
Everett Booe.
In 1913 the Pittsburgh Pirates were trailing in a game by nine runs when Bucs manager Fred Clarke

decided to give two of his rookies some playing time. When the first freshman appeared at the plate, the ump inquired, "Who are you and who are you batting for?"

The rookie replied churlishly: "My name is Riggs and I'm batting for myself!" The umpire was not amused by the display of freshness, and was even less pleased when Riggs ripped the first pitch for a single.

Manager Clarke then dispatched his next rookie pinch hitter to the plate, whereupon the umpire bellowed "What's *your* name and who are you batting for?

The frightened rookie sheepishly replied, "Boo!"

Enraged by the apparent impudence, the umpire shouted, "Get out of the game! Get out of the park! Get out of my sight before I murder you!" The frightened rookie fled from the scene.

It took ten minutes for Clarke to explain that the name of his pinch hitter was none other than Everett Booe. He finally won his point, and Booe returned to the plate for his turn at bat.

WHEN DID THE METS FIRST WIN THE PENNANT?

1884.

That's right, the year was 1884. In 1883 the American Association expanded from six teams to eight and established a New York franchise, playing at the Polo Grounds. The team was called the New York Metropolitans, or Mets for short.

The original Mets were led by Jim Mutrie, who also is credited with naming the Giants. The 1883 Mets were a weak club. Jackson Nelson led the club in batting with a .305 mark. The team finished fourth, barely over .500, although they drew well.

The Mets shared the Polo Grounds with the Giants, who forced the new team to play only morning games, thus affording themselves the more lucrative afternoon market. Nevertheless, in 1884 the Mets rose to the top of the American Association. First baseman Dave Orr hit .534 to lead the Association in batting. Pitchers Tim Keefe and Jack Lynch not only won 37 games each, but also had earned-run averages of 2.29 and 2.64, respectively. After the Mets ran away with the pennant, manager Mutrie challenged the National League to a "series of five games for the championship of the United States and $1,000 a side, under the following conditions: two games to be played under National League rules and two under American Association Rules; the manner and place of playing a fifth game to be decided thereafter."

So the series was to be a best-of-five affair matching Mutrie's Mets and Frank Bancroft's mighty Providence Grays, who boasted an outstanding pitcher in 60-game-winner Charlie "Old Hoss" Radbourn. Radbourn was backed up by center fielder Paul Hines, who hit .302. The rest of the team hit under .270, which proved that Old Hoss really carried the Grays. In the play-off, Radbourn won all three games from the Mets, 6–0, 3–1, and 12–2. (He made it to Baseball's Hall of Fame in 1939.)

A year later the Mets fell apart, finishing seventh (next to last) in both 1885 and 1886. The stars, the pitchers, and the audience were all gone. In 1887 the old New York Mets played their last game in front of 25 people, at which point the franchise was moved to Kansas City.

AMONG THE MOST IGNOMINIOUS REC-
ORDS IN MODERN BASEBALL IS THE WORST
LOSING STREAK. WHAT TEAM IS RESPON-
SIBLE FOR THAT INFAMOUS MARK?

The Philadelphia Phillies of 1961 struggled
through a 23-game losing streak in the month of
August. Such grandiose ineptitude was but one game
short of breaking the all-time record for a losing
streak, set by the 1899 Cleveland Naps, who lost 24
straight.

The Phils' horrendous skein began on July 29,
1961, with a 4–3 loss to the San Francisco Giants;
Orlando Cepeda's grand slam put away the game in
the very first inning. For the next three weeks, Phillie
pitchers Jim Owens, Chris Short, Art Mahaffey, Frank
Sullivan, Johnny Buzhardt, and an ailing Robin Roberts watched their earned-run averages balloon and
their won–loss records become lopsided.

On August 12, 1961, Vinegar Bend Mizell's shutout lifted the Pirates past the Phillies and broke the
all-time Phil record for the longest losing streak. Four
days later, the Phillies tied the modern National
League record for losses (19 games), previously held
by the 1904 Boston Braves and the 1914 Cincinnati
Reds. The next day, the Phils lost their 20th in a row
to the Braves to tie the all-time losing-streak mark of
the 1906 Boston Red Sox and the 1916 and 1943
Philadelphia Athletics.

On August 20th, Johnny Buzhardt, the last Phillie to win previously, pitched against the Milwaukee
Braves. The Phillies scored seven runs to end the losing streak. They returned to Philadelphia and a tumul-
tuous reception—something that never happened to
the Cleveland Naps of 1899. After their 24-game los-

ing streak, the Naps lost their fans and played to an audience of groundskeepers, sportswriters, and vendors. A year later the team disbanded.

DO YOU RECALL THE PITCHER WHO STAGED A HOLDOUT WITH THE APPROVAL OF HIS OWNER?

Bob Feller.

Bill Veeck, the master showman who then owned the Cleveland Indians, liked to get publicity any way he could. One scheme involved "contract talks" with Feller, the Indians' ace pitcher. Feller would come in to contract talks in Veeck's office from time to time during the winter, ostensibly to talk contract. Actually, Veeck and Feller would discuss everything but contract. When the chat was over, Feller would leave, telling newsmen that his differences with Veeck were wide but could, in time, be settled. The press then would speculate at length about the Veeck-Feller hassle.

When spring approached, Veeck would invite Feller to his office. The pitcher and owner would write down on separate slips of paper their ideas on the salary, then they would reveal the numbers and split the difference.

HOW DID BABE RUTH RUIN A WORLD SERIES FOR THE NEW YORK YANKEES?

The 1926 World Series pitted the St. Louis Cardinals against the Yankees and went the full seven games. In the decisive seventh game, the

Yankees trailed, 3–2, when with two outs in the ninth, Ruth drew a walk from pitcher Grover Cleveland "Ol' Pete" Alexander. Sluggers Bob Meusel and Lou Gehrig were on deck, but neither had a chance to score Ruth, because the Babe was thrown out trying to steal second base, ending the Series.

ALTHOUGH ABNER DOUBLEDAY GETS MOST OF THE CREDIT FOR INVENTING THE GAME OF BASEBALL, ALEXANDER CARTWRIGHT FORMULATED THE FIRST SET OF PLAYING RULES FOR BASEBALL IN 1845. CAN YOU NAME ANY OF THE RULES HE PRODUCED?

Cartwright ruled that the game would end at 21 runs, the ball would have to be pitched underhanded, a batter could only take one base when the ball was hit out of the infield, and every ball caught on a bounce became an out, including foul balls. In addition, he suggested that three outs comprise an inning.

FOR THE FIRST FEW YEARS OF ORGANIZED BASEBALL, THE PITCHER WAS ALLOWED TO THROW THE BALL UNDERHANDED ONLY. WHEN DID THE OVERHAND PITCH BECOME LEGAL?

In 1884 several rule changes were made. One was that a pitcher could throw overhand. Among the other rules written that year was one calling for six balls to make a walk (lowered from seven) and one restricting a pitcher to taking only one step before delivering the pitch.

WHEN AND WHERE WAS THE FIRST NIGHT GAME PLAYED?
At Crosley Field in Cincinnati, between the Pittsburgh Pirates and the Cincinnati Reds, on May 24, 1935.

WHEN JOE DIMAGGIO HIT SAFELY IN 56 CONSECUTIVE GAMES, HE BROKE BOTH THE NATIONAL AND AMERICAN LEAGUE MARKS. NAME THE HOLDERS OF THESE PREVIOUS RECORDS.
DiMaggio broke marks that previously were held by George Sisler and Rogers Hornsby. Hornsby set the National League record in 1924 by hitting safely in 33 straight games while playing for the St. Louis Cardinals. Sisler, playing for the St. Louis Browns in 1922, hit safely in 41 games.

ON AUGUST 18, 1967, GIFTED BOSTON RED SOX OUTFIELDER TONY CONIGLIARO WAS HIT IN THE HEAD BY A PITCH THAT NEARLY ENDED HIS LIFE AND HASTENED THE END OF HIS CAREER. WHO THREW THAT PITCH?
Jack Hamilton of the California Angels, in the bottom of the fourth inning at Fenway Park, Boston.

Conigliaro came to bat against hard-throwing Hamilton. On the first pitch, Conigliaro was hit and suffered a linear fracture of the left cheekbone and a dislocated jaw.

Tony attempted a comeback in 1968 but he was only a shadow of his former self.

WHEN WAS THE MOST VALUABLE PLAYER AWARD FIRST PRESENTED?

In 1922 the American League voted to present an award to its outstanding player. A special committee selected George Sisler of the St. Louis Browns as the first MVP. Two years later, the National League initiated the MVP. Dazzy Vance of the Brooklyn Dodgers was selected as the top National Leaguer of 1924.

FOR THE FIRST 12 YEARS OF ITS EXISTENCE, THE CY YOUNG AWARD WAS AWARDED TO THE BEST PITCHER IN THE MAJORS. EVENTUALLY, IT WAS DECIDED TO PRESENT A PITCHING PRIZE IN EACH LEAGUE. WHEN DID THIS HAPPEN AND WHO WERE THE WINNERS THAT YEAR?

In 1967, after Sandy Koufax of the Los Angeles Dodgers had won the Cy Young Award for the third time, the major leagues voted to give two awards. Named as the best pitchers in 1967 were Jim Lonborg of the Boston Red Sox and Mike McCormick of the San Francisco Giants.

ONE OF THE MOST BIZARRE OFF-THE-FIELD EPISODES IN BASEBALL HISTORY INVOLVED THE SHOOTING OF A PHILADELPHIA PHILLIES FIRST BASEMAN IN 1949. DO YOU KNOW HOW IT CAME ABOUT?

A woman named Ruth Ann Steinhagen claimed she was an ardent fan of Eddie Waitkus and that she went to see him play whenever she could. Yet it was later learned that she had planned to kill Waitkus for two years—in her own words, in order to "relieve my tension."

On June 15, 1949, Steinhagen rented a room at the Edgewater Beach Hotel on Chicago's North Side, where the Phillies stayed when they played in Chicago. Miss Steinhagen wrote a note to Waitkus, a bachelor, and gave a bellboy five dollars to deliver it to him. According to one wire-service report, the note was "enticing." Steinhagen admitted that the note suggested that she had to discuss an "extremely important" matter with him. Waitkus arrived at her room around midnight. Then a shot pierced the night.

Waitkus was wounded severely and missed the rest of the season. However, he returned the following year and batted .284 with the pennant-winning Phillies. In a career that spanned 11 years, Waitkus played a total of 1,140 games with the Cubs, Phillies, and Orioles. His lifetime average was .285.

Steinhagen, who had suffered a nervous breakdown in December 1948, was judged insane by a criminal-court jury and was sent to Kankakee (Illinois) State Hospital. She eventually was released, at which time she said that she wanted to go to work at the state hospital as an occupational therapist.

Waitkus applied for workmen's compensation of $3,500, claiming his visit to Miss Steinhagen's room came under the category of "endeavoring to promote good-will for his employer." The Pennsylvania Workmen's Compensation Board rejected his claim. In its decision, the board explained that it was clear that Waitkus had been carrying out a "private enterprise in which he voluntarily engaged for personal reasons."

HOW DID MICKEY OWEN BECOME ONE OF THE MOST INFAMOUS "GOATS" IN WORLD SERIES ANNALS?

"It couldn't, perhaps, have happened anywhere else on earth. But it did happen yesterday in Brooklyn. . . ." wrote John Drebinger in *The New York Times* of what was one of the most notorious blunders in World Series history. The date was October 5, 1941; the place, Ebbets Field, Brooklyn. The New York Yankees were playing the Brooklyn Dodgers. It had been a strange day on and off the field. In the stands a fire had broken out; no one was injured, but nerves were ruffled. On the field the Brooklyn Dodgers were playing in their first World Series since 1920 and they were within one strike of tying the mighty Yankees and the 1941 Classic at two games apiece. The score was 4–3 when Brooklyn right-handed reliever Hugh Casey delivered a three-and-two-with-two-outs pitch, and the Yankee's Tommy Henrich swung and missed. For a brief moment the euphoric Brooklyn fans rejoiced. A world championship was within striking distance for the Beloved Bums.

But the momentary joy turned to anguish and frustration when Dodger catcher Mickey Owen allowed the ball to slip from his grasp. By the time the normally sure-handed Owen retrieved the ball, Henrich already had crossed first base. What followed was a nightmare for the Dodgers and most of the 33,813 Flatbush Faithful. Joe DiMaggio of the Yankees followed with a single and then Charlie Keller smashed a double. Casey was obviously unnerved, but Dodgers' manager Leo Durocher made no attempt to calm his pitcher. Nor did Durocher have anyone up in the bullpen as the Yankees rally continued. Bill Dickey walked and Joe Gordon doubled. By the time the dust had cleared, the Yankees were ahead, 7–4. They won the game and took a three-games-to-one lead in the series, which they annexed the next day.

The players were no less astonished than those who had witnessed the game from the stands. "Well," said Joe DiMaggio, "they say everything happens in Brooklyn!" Many Yankees were pleased that Owen had been the goat. Owen's harsh slide into Yankees' shortstop Phil Rizzuto during game two had left Rizzuto's knees bandaged and inspired a barrage of catcalls from the Yankee's bench.

Meanwhile, Owen and Casey refrained from comment. Some critics insist that Casey confused Owen by throwing a spitball on the last pitch.

Whatever the cause, the effect of the Casey-Owen miscue left a permanent scar on the Dodgers' psyche.

And of course, the episode inspired suitable prose. The next day, *"Casey in the Box,"* authored by Meyer Berger, appeared in *The New York Times*. The last stanza said it all:

> Oh somewhere North of Harlem the sun is shining bright
> Bands are playing in the Bronx and up there hearts are light

116

In Hunts Point men are laughing, on the Con-
    course children shout
But there is no joy in Flatbush. Fate had knocked
    their Casey out.

RONALD REAGAN ONCE PORTRAYED
ON THE SCREEN A GREAT MAJOR LEAGUE
PITCHER. WHO WAS THE PITCHER AND
WHAT WAS THE NAME OF THE FILM?

The pitcher was Grover Cleveland Alexander
and the Warner Brothers' film was called *The Win-*
ning Team.

Reagan made the movie in 1950, along with
Doris Day and Frank Lovejoy. Reagan affectionately
recalled that his future wife, Nancy, frequently was
on the set for the filming. "Nancy," said Reagan, "had
inherited a love for baseball from her mother, Edie,
a Broadway actress who refused to go to the hospital
on the day that Nancy was due, the Fourth of July,
because she wanted to go to a doubleheader that day.
She went and had Nancy later."

To help lend authenticity to *The Winning Team,*
Warner Brothers hired a dozen big-leaguers to work
alongside Reagan. "I asked Nancy if it would be all
right if I gave her an autographed baseball instead
of a mink coat as a wedding present," Reagan recalled.
"She said it sure was. I got the players to autograph a
ball and present it to her. She was thrilled. It was a
fine film, I think. And I especially treasure its memory because it was the last film I made before I ran
off to marry Nancy."

WHEN DID A BALL PARK GO UP IN SMOKE WHILE A FIGHT TOOK PLACE ON THE DIAMOND?

During a bitterly fought game between the Baltimore Orioles and the Boston Braves on May 16, 1894, in Boston, the Orioles' truculent third baseman, John J. "Muggsy" McGraw, had antagonized several members of the home team. The hostility multiplied in intensity until finally McGraw became embroiled in a fight with Boston's equally belligerent first baseman, Tommy "Foghorn" Tucker.

As the players bloodied themselves on the field, the frenzied fans worked themselves into a fever pitch in the stands. As it happened a gang of hoodlums watching the game from the bleachers had chose to set their seats on fire. What began as a prank degenerated into a disaster. Within minutes the blaze spread to other parts of the stadium, eventually burning down not only the ball park but 170 other buildings as well. According to one estimate, the property damage resulting from the ball-park fire ran into the millions of dollars!

A WORLD SERIES ONCE WAS DELAYED BECAUSE OF A PLAYERS' STRIKE. CAN YOU REMEMBER WHEN?

During the 1918 season the salaries of ball players were, on the whole, exceptionally low, and gripes about conditions were heard throughout the rank-and-file of all major league teams. By the time the World Series between the Chicago Cubs and Boston Red Sox had begun, there was massive discontent among the players. This malaise spread as small crowds attended the first four games of the Series. After the fourth game, the players realized that they were going to get a small cut of the World Series pie, so they called a strike prior to the fifth game, refusing to return unless they got more money. Representatives from both the National and American league teams quickly convened and finally hammered out an agreement with Ban Johnson, who represented the club owners. The players thus ended the only sitdown strike in World Series history.

A WELL-KNOWN FASTBALL PITCHER ONCE INADVERTENTLY CAUSED INJURY TO HIS MOTHER DURING A BALL GAME. WHO WAS HE?

Bob "Rapid Robert" Feller had become one of the foremost pitchers in the majors by the end of the 1930s. Hurling for the Cleveland Indians, Feller was was the toast of the American League. On Mother's Day, 1939, Bob invited his Mom to watch him pitch against the Chicago White Sox at Comiskey Park. Mrs. Feller accepted the invitation and went directly from her Iowa farm to the Windy City.

Her son was at the top of his game as Mrs. Feller proudly watched him mow down one Chicago player after another. Suddenly, Bob wound up and burned one down the middle. The Chicago batsman swung late and fouled the ball into the stands. As 45,000 fans watched in awe, the ball careened off the head of a woman spectator. The fan just happened to be Bob Feller's mother.

A ONE-ARMED PLAYER STARRED IN THE MAJORS FOR ALMOST A DECADE. WHO WAS HE?

Hugh Daly was a pitcher who won 15 games in his rookie season and 26 games in his sophomore year in the bigs. Over a span of eight seasons, Daly once pitched a no-hit, no-run game and on another occasion struck out 19 men in a game. So adroit was Daly that on days he was not on the mound he could play either shortstop or second base.

NAME THE FORMER LONG ISLAND UNIVERSITY BASKETBALL PLAYER WHO FIGURED PROMINENTLY IN ONE OF THE MOST FREAKISH ACCIDENTS IN WORLD SERIES HISTORY.

Marius Russo.

Russo figured in yet another episode in the saga of the Brooklyn Dodgers and the New York Yankees. Russo, a first-rate basketeer, was also an ace on the 1941 Yankees' pitching staff. In the third game of the 1941 World Series between Brooklyn and New York, Russo faced Freddie Fitzsimmons of the Dodgers. Russo and Fitzsimmons were locked in a 0–0 tie when Russo came to bat in the top of the seventh inning.

The Yankees had a runner on second but Fitzsimmons seemed in control of his pitching. It seemed the game would go on until someone cracked. Finally, someone did crack. Russo smashed a wicked line drive that caromed off Fitzsimmons's left leg just above the knee. The ball was deflected up in the air, where shortstop Pee Wee Reese caught for the third out. Fitzsimmons also was out of the game, as well as the rest of the Series. His kneecap was all but shattered. The Dodgers did get to Russo for one run, but the Yankees got two and won the game, 2–1.

TED "THE SPLENDID SPLINTER" WILLIAMS BATTED .406 DURING THE 1941 SEASON FOR THE BOSTON RED SOX, YET HE FAILED TO LEAD THE AMERICAN LEAGUE IN HITS. WHO DID?

Cecil Travis of the Washington Senators had 218 hits in 608 at bats for a .359 batting average. Travis was a shortstop–third baseman and, obviously a super hitter who batted .314 in a career that spanned 12 years. Ted Williams finished fourth in hits during the 1941 campaign. Ahead of him were Travis, Jeff Heath of the Cleveland Indians, who had 199 hits and a batting average of .340; and Joe DiMaggio of the New York Yankees, who had 193 hits in 541 at bats for an average of .357. DiMaggio also hit 30 home runs and had 125 runs batted in. Williams hit 37 homers and 120 runs batted in to go with his .406 average. He had 185 hits in 456 at bats to tie for fourth in hits with Luke Appling of the Chicago White Sox, who had 185 hits in 592 at bats for an average of .312.

LONG BEFORE JACKIE ROBINSON BROKE BASEBALL'S COLOR BARRIER AND BECAME THE FIRST BLACK TO PLAY IN THE MAJOR LEAGUES, ATTEMPTS WERE MADE TO ENABLE BLACKS TO PLAY IN THE NATIONAL AND AMERICAN LEAGUE. DO YOU RECALL

THE FAMOUS SINGER WHO LED SUCH A CRUSADE?

Operatic star Paul Robeson.

During the 1943 season, the Negro Giants baseball team defeated a team of major and minor league stars in an exhibition game, 4–3. Satchel Paige, the excellent black pitcher, struck out 14 batters. With this in mind, a delegation of blacks headed by Robeson, met with Baseball Commissioner Kenesaw Mountain Landis and club owners during the winter baseball meetings. Robeson argued passionately for the admission of blacks to organized baseball.

The owners told Robeson that the American public would not tolerate blacks in the majors. Robeson, who had been an All-American football player at Rutgers, was then starring in *Othello* on Broadway. "They once said that America would never stand for my playing *Othello* with a white cast, but it is the triumph of my life," said Robeson.

After listening to the blacks, the Lords of baseball tacitly agreed to keep Negroes out of their leagues. *The Sporting News* reported: "The Negro delegates were told by Landis that there was no baseball rule against the signing of members of their race and there the matter was left, just where it had been."

RAY HAYWORTH WAS A MAJOR LEAGUE CATCHER FOR 15 YEARS. GUS MANCUSO WAS A MAJOR LEAGUE CATCHER FOR 17 YEARS. THEIR KID BROTHERS WOUND UP ON THE SAME TEAM IN 1944—BOTH AS CATCHERS. WHO WERE THEY?

Myron "Red" Hayworth and Frank Mancuso.

According to St. Louis Browns historian William B. Mead, "Red Hayworth was a poor hitter but a good receiver, although he had some difficulty catching pop flies . . . Frank Mancuso joined the Army in 1942, was commissioned a lieutenant and volunteered for the paratroops. After four successful jumps, Mancuso was almost ready for combat duty. On his fifth jump, however, he fell from the airplane head-first by mistake. His legs caught in the lines, and when he landed he broke a leg and wrenched his back. The back injury was so bad that Mancuso could neither stay in the Army nor, as the Browns soon discovered, look straight up for a pop fly."

AFTER BEING ACCEPTED INTO THE UNITED STATES ARMY AIR CORPS, A WASHINGTON SENATORS' STAR ACTUALLY DIVED HIS PLANE OVER GRIFFITH STADIUM WHILE A GAME WAS ON. WHO WAS HE?

Buddy Lewis, the Senators third baseman, who served more than three years as an Army Air Corps transport pilot.

Lewis admitted that he loved flying even more than playing baseball. And he did love his baseball. After earning his pilot's wings, Lewis was stationed at Lawson Field in Georgia. "As part of our training," Lewis recalled, "they'd say, 'Take a crew and go to any city you want to on the weekends. Let us know what you're doing and when you're going back, but go.' I guess I spent every weekend away.

"Once, I took a planeload into Washington on one of these trips in 1943, and I went to Griffith Stadium and I spoke to everybody I knew. I told them I was coming by with my plane; I had landed at Andrews Air Base, and I had to leave to go back to Georgia late in the afternoon. I broke every rule in the book. I knew where Griffith Stadium was. There was a game on, and I flew straight there and made a dive over the stadium. I was down low enough so I could almost read the letters on the uniforms. George Case told me later that he was the batter, and he threw his bat up in the air. I took off. I knew I was in the wrong, and I expected to be reprimanded. But there were no repercussions. I was surprised the people in the Pentagon didn't read about it in the paper and get in touch with my commanding officer."

NOT ONLY WAS THIS ATHLETE THE FIRST MAJOR LEAGUER TO ENLIST IN THE AMERICAN ARMED FORCES IN WORLD WAR I, BUT HE ALSO SERVED IN WORLD WAR II.

Hank Gowdy, who starred for the Boston Braves, was baseball's first contribution to the World War I effort. When World War II began, Gowdy was coaching the Cincinnati Reds and remained as patriotic as he had been in his youth. "I have been the recipient of many honors in my lengthy baseball career," said Gowdy, "and also have been in receipt of honors outside the realm of baseball. But the highest honor of my entire life came through being privileged to wear the United States Army uniform and serve my country in the last war [World War I] in which it was engaged."

Gowdy soon backed up his words: in early 1943, at the age of 53, he enlisted again and was commissioned as a captain in the army.

WHAT PLAYER WON THE 1940 NATIONAL LEAGUE BATTING CHAMPIONSHIP FOR PITTSBURGH BUT WAS CONSIGNED TO THE MINORS WHEN HIS BATTING AVERAGE DROPPED 91 POINTS THE FOLLOWING YEAR.

Debs Garms is the man—but his tale was not all that sad. With the arrival of World War II and a massive exodus of first-liners to the armed forces, big-league teams needed players badly. The St. Louis Cardinals resurrected Garms at the age of 35 in the 1943 season. It proved to be a good move, since Garms helped the Cards to the National League pennant.

AN ABSURD INCIDENT LED TO BOSTON BRAVES OUTFIELDER GEORGE METKOVICH BEING NICKNAMED "CATFISH" AT SPRING TRAINING IN 1940. DO YOU HAVE A CLUE AS TO WHY?

Metkovich liked to fish. One day he caught a three-foot catfish while fishing from a bridge. After landing the prize, the eager Metkovich placed his foot on the catfish's back and then attempted to remove the hook. The traumatized catfish raised a sharp fin that sliced through the crepe sole of Metkovich's shoe and on through most of his foot. So bad was the wound that Metkovich had to have surgery to remove the fin. The rookie's beleaguered manager was Casey Stengel, who remarked to reporters, "I've got a young first baseman by the name of Metkovich who's in the hospital. Do you know how? He was attacked by a catfish!"

George's defenders point out that his mishap was

rivaled in the ridiculous category by the injury to Fat Freddie Fitzsimmons, the New York Giants' pitcher who suffered a severe hand injury when, while rocking on a hotel veranda, he let his hand droop and then rocked over his own fingers!

RON HUNT OWNS ONE OF THE PAINFUL RECORDS IN THE MAJOR LEAGUES. WHAT IS IT?

Most times hit by a pitched ball. Hunt's 243 plunkings constitute a major league standard that has caused Ron many a wince.

A second baseman who started with the New York Mets in 1963, Hunt was traded to the Giants and then to the Expos later in an 11-year career. As for his penchant for being plunked, Hunt said, "Everything worthwhile in life demands a price. Some people give their bodies to science; I give mine to baseball. Actually, a player who lacks certain skills should try to find some way to compensate for his shortcomings. With me it was getting hit by a pitch."

Hunt suffered his most painful year in 1971, when he was hit 50 times. Ron truly gave his body to baseball.

DUKE KENWERTHY HAD A GENUINELY "GOLDEN OPPORTUNITY" WHILE PLAYING SECOND BASE IN THE OLD FEDERAL LEAGUE. DO YOU KNOW WHY?

Kenwerthy, who played for the Kansas City nine, was patroling second base one day when a grounder ricocheted off a pebble and bounced into right field. Disgusted, Kenwerthy picked up the pebble and then did a double take. He noticed a special glint about it, and stuffed the "pebble" in his pocket. That evening he studied the "pebble" and determined that it was actually a piece of gold. Kenwerthy returned to the ball park and dug up the area around his position and found still more gold.

According to the legend, he later bought the ball park and turned second base into a gold mine.

WHO WAS THE HIGHEST-PAID BATBOY IN THE MAJOR LEAGUES?

Eddie Bennett, a hunchback, is regarded as the most famous batboy of all times. Bennett worked for the Chicago White Sox, the Brooklyn Dodgers, and the New York Yankees in the 1920s. Eddie was sought by many teams because he was considered a good-luck charm by the hitters, who would rub his back as they strode to the plate. Bennett often was paid as high as many varsity players.

IN 1978 A JUNIOR HIGH SCHOOL WAS NAMED AFTER AN ACTIVE MAJOR LEAGUER. DO YOU KNOW WHICH ONE?

On February 25, 1978, Abraham Lincoln Junior High School of Lindsay, California, was renamed Steve Garvey Junior High School, in honor of the Los Angeles Dodgers' power-hitting first baseman. Moreover, the school's library was named in honor of Dodgers' manager Tom LaSorda.

Writer Art Hill commented, "In hip Southern California, who wants a school named after some dead guy? Garvey led the Dodgers to a pennant in the previous year; Lincoln hadn't done anything worth talking about for ages. He did save the Union, though. If he hadn't, Garvey, who comes from Florida, might have been a jai alai player."

HEAVYWEIGHT CHAMPION GENTLEMAN JIM CORBETT ONCE TRIED TO DISSUADE HIS BROTHER JOE FROM PLAYING BASEBALL. GUESS WHY?

Jim Corbett tried to dissuade Joe from playing because he believed that "baseball was growing too violent." Fortunately, Joe ignored Jim's advice, and he became a 20-game winner for the Baltimore Orioles in 1897.

WHAT MAJOR EFFECT DID HARRY WRIGHT HAVE ON BASEBALL UNIFORMS?

Harry Wright, an English-born former cricketer, was the playing manager of the first professional ball team, the Cincinnati Red Stockings. Wright's background in cricket led him to design the Red Stockings' uniform as exact replicas of cricket uniforms. As a result, the cricket uniform helped influence the modern baseball uniform.

The sun never sets...

NAME THE MAJOR LEAGUE PLAYER WHOSE SISTER WAS A FENCING GREAT.

Lou Gehrig's sister, Adeline Gehrig, was national women's foil champion in 1920, 1921, 1922, and 1923.

WHAT WAS THE FIRST BASEBALL TEAM TO GO ON A BARNSTORMING TOUR?

A team called the Nationals, comprised of government workers in Washington, D.C., covered 2,400 miles in three weeks following the Civil War, playing ten games in that span. Their only defeat was inflicted by a team representing Rockford, Illinois, whose 17-year-old pitcher went on to acquire fame as a player and then as a manufacturer—none other than Albert Goodwill Spalding.

WHO BOUGHT THE UNITED STATES' FIRST BASEBALL STAMP?

On June 12, 1939, amid the ceremonies marking the opening of baseball's Hall of Fame, Commissioner Kenesaw Mountain Landis pushed three copper pennies through a grille in the Cooperstown (New York) Post Office and received from Postmaster-General James Farley the first commemorative baseball stamp ever issued in the United States.

Wearing a red, white, and blue souvenir baseball cap, Farley dispensed other stamps to baseball executives Will Harridge, Clark Griffith, Ford Frick. Eddie Brannick, the New York Giants' secretary, bought 1,200 of the new stamps.

Farley not only sold the stamps, he also had to

provide souvenir cancellations, and autographs. A neighbor observed Cooperstown Postmaster Mel Bundy standing on the steps and chuckled, "Mel, why don't you go in there and give your boss a hand!"

THE HARRY M. STEVENS COMPANY PROVIDES MOST OF THE NATION'S BALL PARKS WITH PEANUTS, SCORECARDS, AND HOT DOGS, AND HAS DONE SO SINCE THE 1880S. YET THIS ORGANIZATION WAS LAUNCHED BY AN ENGLISHMAN WHO KNEW NOTHING ABOUT BASEBALL. HOW DID STEVENS HAPPEN TO DO IT?

Harry M. Stevens could never explain what prompted him to go to a baseball game, a sport he had never seen before. But one day, while in Columbus, Ohio, Harry went to the ball park. The game was incomprehensible to him, and all his questions to surrounding fans about the names of the players (which were unknown to many), went unanswered.

The following day, Stevens, a Shakespearean scholar and book salesman, visited the offices of the Columbus club and obtained exclusive rights for selling a card listing all the players' names, with an empty space for fans to score the game's highlights. The next day Stevens was selling advertising space on the scorecard.

In order to get information about other aspects of the game, at his next game, he sat in the bleachers with a large sack of peanuts, trading the peanuts for answers to questions.

By 1910 he had concessionaires selling hot dogs and beer, as well as scorecards, across the continent.

But to his death in the 1930s, Harry Stevens could never say exactly why he went to see that baseball game in Columbus, Ohio.

SOME OF THE WORST BRAWLS IN BASEBALL HAVE INVOLVED THE NEW YORK YANKEES AND BOSTON RED SOX. CAN YOU RECALL ANY OF THE INCIDENTS?

The Red Sox and the Yankees several times have nearly launched a diamond war. On May 30, 1938, at Yankee Stadium, for example, Boston lefthander Archie McKain had been throwing too close to Jake Powell, a Yankee outfielder. Powell rushed to the mound but never made it. Red Sox shortstop Joe Cronin intercepted Powell and started swinging in defense of McKain. Cronin, however, was not announced as a "pinch hitter" before cooler heads prevailed.

Fenway Park was the scene of another Sox-Yanks clash, in 1952. Only this time, Billy Martin of the Bronx Bombers and Jimmy Piersall of the Red Sox couldn't wait for the game to begin. They went at it before the players even took the field.

Beanballs played a role in Yanks-Sox Brawl III, at Yankee Stadium in 1967. In the course of the game, New York hurler Thad Tillotson hit Boston third baseman Joe Foy with a pitch. Retribution came in the form of a Jim Lonborg fastball. The Yankees' bench emptied and a brouhaha ensued. The main bout took place between Boston's Rico Petrocelli and the Yankees' Joe Pepitone.

Home plate at Fenway was transformed into another war zone in 1973, all because Gene Michael of the Yankees missed a suicide squeeze bunt. The runner from third, Thurman Munson, a catcher by trade, saw Carleton Fisk, Boston's pride of home plate, catch the ball and brace himself for a collision between the two best young catchers in the American League. Munson was ready too—with elbows way up. BANG! Fisk absorbed the full impact of Munson's 188 pounds, landed on his American Express card, and came up swinging.

Both Munson and Michael then attacked Fisk, leaving him with a bruised eye and a scratched face.

"The Yankees and Red Sox have played this way since baseball was invented," says Fisk. "I must admit we get out there against them with a lot of intensity. Sometimes we get carried away a little."

On a warm Thursday night in May 1976, Boston's flaky left-handed pitcher Bill Lee almost had to be carried away himself, following a bench-clearing brawl with the hated New Yorkers in the refurbished Yankee Stadium. The defending American League champs trailed the first-place Yankees by six games as the two clubs began a four-game weekend series.

In the bottom half of the sixth, New York was threatening to add to its precarious 1–0 lead, with Lou Piniella on second base and Graig Nettles on first. The batter, Otto Velez, lined a Lee fastball into right field. Dwight Evans, who earlier had thrown out Fred Stanley at home plate, again faced the challenge of retiring a baserunner at home. As the medium-fast Piniella chugged around third base with the green light from coach Dick Howser, the charging Evans scooped up the ball, reared back, and fired an accurate one-hop throw to catcher Fisk. The Sox' talented backstop received the skidding throw on the first-base side of the plate, turned on his knees to meet the sliding

Yankee runner, and tagged him out. But it didn't end there.

Piniella thought the ball had been jarred loose by the collision and tried desperately to kick it away so that umpire Terry Cooney would see it. But instead of the ball, Piniella inadvertently kicked Fisk.

Having suffered several painful groin injuries on previous plays like this one, Fisk took exception to Piniella's actions. He tagged him with the ball a second time—only harder, and in the jaw. Lou grabbed the catcher's chest protector to get out from under him and Fisk rapped him again on the chin; this time with the ball in his right hand. Then the real donnybrook began.

At that moment, Boston first baseman Carl Yastrzemski and Yankee on-deck hitter Sandy Alomar raced to home plate to act as peacemakers. The rest of the players figured Yastrzemski and Alomar were going to fight, too, so they stormed the diamond with fists cocked.

Bill Lee was the next "outsider" to join the fracas, followed by the Yankees' Velez and Graig Nettles, who put both his arms around the Boston pitcher to try and drag him off the pile-up of players.

"I heard him [Lee] yelling that his shoulder was hurt," Nettles recalled. "If I wanted to punch him right there I could have killed him, but I didn't. At that point I just wanted to break it up."

Meanwhile, New York outfielder Mickey Rivers, who also had charged out of the dugout to lend physical support, jumped Lee from behind, dragged him to the ground with a hammerlock, and uncorked a number of vicious hammerlike punches in a windmilling manner. With Boston's ace left-hander lying on the turf in pain, Nettles tried to explain to a few of Lee's teammates that he only wanted to get him off the pile. Suddenly Lee got up, walked over to Nettles and delivered a barrage of invective that made the Yankee third baseman sorry that he even attempted to make peace. At one point Lee told Nettles, "If you ever hurt my shoulder again, I'll kill you." That was all the mild-mannered Nettles had to hear.

"He started screaming at me like he was crazy," Graig said. "There were tears in his eyes. He told me he was going to get me, and that's when he started coming after me. I wasn't going to back off any more."

Nettles then connected with a right cross to the eye that decked Lee. They finished their private war on the ground. By now the pain in Lee's shoulder was excruciating. Red Sox trainer Charley Moss rushed to the fallen pitcher and escorted him to the dressing room. It turned out to be Lee's last appearance in uniform for about six weeks.

The rest of the casualty list read like a typical National Football League injury report. Carl Yastrzemski bruised his foot, and Lou Piniella bruised his hand, but miraculously, the injury-prone Fisk escaped unscathed.

Basebrawling has not been confined to Yankees-Red Sox encounters, however. Several ugly incidents took place between other teams in both play-off and regular-season encounters.

Pitcher Juan Marichal of the San Francisco Giants once took exception to Dodger catcher John Roseboro's return throw to Sandy Koufax while Marichal was batting. The Dominican Dandy thought the throw was too close to his head, so he turned around and swung his bat at Roseboro's head like he was cutting a log with an axe.

The "RoseBud" incident in the 1973 National

League play-off was an illustration of one man's struggle against an entire city: the man was Pete Rose and the city was New York. The Mets and the Cincinnati Reds were tied in the best-of-five series at a game apiece when the clubs met in game three at Shea Stadium. The Mets were breezing along with a seven-run lead in the top of the fifth, when Rose slashed a one-out single to the outfield.

The next batter, Joe Morgan, hit a hard bouncer to first base. Met first baseman John Milner fired the ball to shortstop Bud Harrelson, covering at second base. As Harrelson was completing the double-play throw to first, Rose slid hard into the 165-pound shortstop knocking him flying. What ensued was a spirited but hardly convincing wrestling match between the two players.

The fans got into the act, too, throwing empty beer bottles at Pete Rose in his left-field position until a contingent of Mets including Tom Seaver, Cleon Jones, Rusty Staub, Willie Mays, and manager Yogi Berra, asked the fans to desist under threat of a forfeit.

WHO IS THE "JOE" OF BASEBALL'S VENERABLE QUOTE: "SAY IT AIN'T SO, JOE?"

"Shoeless Joe" Jackson, the left fielder of the 1919 "Black Sox" is the man.

Jackson was one of the prime figures in the notorious Black Sox scandal and was one of eight players banned for life from big league baseball by Commissioner Kenesaw Mountain Landis.

The Black Sox scandal was a huge pimple on the face of professional baseball in 1921—a blemish that, fortunately, soon was medicated by the stern ruling of Judge Landis and the glamour of home-run-hitting Babe Ruth. But though the pimple was removed, a scar remained, and to this day, that scar is best symbolized by an episode that transpired late in September 1920, when "Shoeless" Joe Jackson spilled his story. The *Chicago Herald and Examiner* summed it up:

"As Jackson departed from the grand jury room, a small boy clutched at his sleeve and tagged along after him.

" 'Say it ain't so, Joe,' he pleaded. 'Say it ain't so.'

" 'Yes, kid, I'm afraid it is,' Jackson replied.

" 'Well, I never would've thought it,' the boy said."

A ROOKIE ALMOST SINGLEHANDEDLY WON THE 1931 WORLD SERIES FOR THE ST. LOUIS CARDINALS OVER THE PHILADELPHIA ATHLETICS. WHO WAS HE?

Pepper Martin.

During the regular National League season, Martin hit a robust .300, but more significantly, he popularized a leaping, head-first slide that complemented his brazen deportment on the basepaths. Philadelphia writers, however, warned that in the Series, Martin's gambles with the throwing arm of Athletics catcher Mickey Cochrane would hasten his departure for the minors. Few challenged Cochrane's arm and lived to say that they were safe.

The question, as the World Series opened at Sportsman's Park in St. Louis, was whether manager Street would manacle Martin, forcing him to play a more conservative game in deference to Cochrane and the A's.

The answer was not long in coming. With Philadelphia leading, 4–2, in the sixth inning, Martin singled, and then took on the mighty Cochrane. Getting the jump on Lefty Grove's windup, Pepper sped to second, sliding in head-first inches ahead of Cochrane's too-late throw. The Cardinals' crowd roared with delight, but Martin was stranded as the rest of the St. Louis lineup fell prey to Grove's hard-nosed hurling. Philadelphia won the game, 6–2, to take a one-game lead in the Series. If nothing else, Pepper Martin had served notice that he would run with abandon, and now, unexpectedly, the A's and Mickey Cochrane were on the defensive.

In game two, Martin taunted Cochrane by taking extraordinarily long leads off second, although no one in the rapt audience dared believe that he would actually go from second to third. Perhaps Cochrane shared the thoughts of the crowd because he was caught flat-handed when Pepper *did* make his mad dash, snaring third base in another flying slide. A minute later Martin scored the game's first run on a sacrifice fly.

Reassured by the one-run lead, the Cards smote the mighty Athletics for seven consecutive innings without a run. However, they had not provided more runs. As the last of the seventh began, the Cards were nursing a 1–0 margin. It was time for the rookie Martin to traumatize the Athletics further. Pepper launched his one-man attack with a single and, with the audacity of a pirate, he stole yet another base off Cochrane. Martin moved to third on an infield out. It was a trying moment for Cochrane as Martin crept away from third.

What followed was one of the most pulsating plays in the World Series history. The two redbirds perched on the bat on Martin's chest-crest seemed to jump up and down as Pepper zig-zagged along the path from third to home. In the Athletics' dugout, venerable manager Connie Mack tried to determine whether adversary Charles Street would order a full swing or a subtler ploy.

Pepper and friends decided to push their luck with the law of averages. The Cardinals' strategy was to lure Cochrane from behind the plate with a bunt, so that by the time he had fielded the ball, he would be too far out of position to tag the onrushing Martin. The "squeeze play" could have been printed in a baseball textbook, it worked so splendidly. Cochrane was lured from his position by the bunt; he nabbed the ball, all right, but Martin was moving at speeds of upward of 25 miles per hour by the time the frustrated Philadelphia catcher could make a move with the ball. Martin slid safely into home plate, feet-first, using his right hand as a balancing cushion.

The St. Louis crowd of 35,947 set new records for decibel counts as the "safe" sign was flashed and Martin scored the Cardinals' second run. More than that, the crowd was toasting their marvelous new rookie, who in two games had accumulated five hits and three stolen bases and had delivered on a squeeze play against baseball's finest catcher. Allowing only three hits in nine innings, the Cards won the game, 2–0.

The Series was now tied at one game apiece. In game three, the Athletics went with crack pitcher Lefty Grove. But Martin came through with a single and a double, scoring two runs. The final score was 2–0, St. Louis.

The Philadelphia brain trust immediately huddled to find an answer to the Pepper Martin problem. Connie Mack figured that the only pitcher who might handcuff Martin at this point was the redoubtable George Earnshaw. Mack was wise in selecting Earnshaw, but wrong in believing that he could thwart the irrepressible Martin. Pepper smacked a single in the fifth—and then stole second—and doubled in the eighth. The trouble for St. Louis was that those were the only hits off Earnshaw, who allowed not a run while the A's gathered one in the first and a pair in the sixth for a 3–0 victory.

With the Series tied at two games apiece, two interesting developments were taking place. First, despite their comeback, the A's realized that the Cardinals were a considerably improved team over the one they had faced in 1930; and second, the reason for that improvement was none other than Pepper Martin. Mack's man designated to stop him in game five on October 7, 1931, was Waite Hoyt. It was a poor choice right from the first inning. Up at the plate for the first time, Martin was asked to advance a runner on third base. When Hoyt released the ball, Martin took a good look at it and hung it on a vicious line to the wall in left center. It wasn't a double—although it sounded like one—but a devastating out that brought in the first run of the game.

So much for the "stop Martin" strategy. The Cards' rookie had become so appealing that even partisan Philadelphia fans cheered every time he came to bat—which was not the case in the Athletics' dugout. No matter which defense Mack erected, Martin deduced a method for outwitting the master. In the fourth inning, Mack ordered the infield way back in anticipation of a hard smash; so Pepper merely laid down a bunt and ran it out for a single. In the sixth, with the A's alert for a bunt, Pepper powered a drive into the bleachers for a two-run homer. That added two runs to the Cardinals' lead, making it 3–0. The A's finally scratched one run off Hallahan in the bottom of the seventh, but Martin returned to produce yet another hit and run batted in, and ultimately, the Cards danced off with a 5–1 win, and a three-games-to-two series advantage.

"Martin had already come up with the greatest performance by a rookie in World Series history," wrote one newspaperman. The Cards eventually won the Series in the seventh game.

WHO WAS THE WHITE BASEBALL STAR CONSIDERED LARGELY RESPONSIBLE FOR KEEPING BLACKS OUT OF MAJOR LEAGUE BASEBALL?

The culprit was Adrian "Cap" Anson.

On an April morning in 1887, Anson's team, the Chicago White Stockings, were to play Newark of the Eastern League. It loomed as an especially interesting game, since the widely acclaimed Anson, captain of the White Stockings, would be facing George Stovey, Newark's nonpareil pitcher.

There were several unusual credits in Stovey's dossier, not the least of which was his record of having won 35 games during the previous season. That was the central theme of all saloon soliloquies about Stovey. Occasionally, his boosters would touch on other aspects of his life, such as the fact that George was a foreigner—a Canadian by birth—and a Negro. Because of his light skin, Stovey was not so obviously a Negro as, say, Jackie Robinson was. But there was no mistaking that Stovey was a black man. When Cap Anson made that discovery, he walked off the field rather than allow himself and his White Stockings the "ignominy" of playing against a Negro.

Anson didn't realize it at the time, but he had just closed and locked the door of big-league baseball on the black man. "His walk," observed black author John Holway, "set a pattern that would last for exactly sixty years. One by one the blacks were eased out of organized baseball."

Had Anson treated Stovey with the consummate respect that Brooklyn Dodgers' captain Harold "Pee Wee" Reese accorded Jackie Robinson, it is quite possible, if not probable, that blacks would have been naturally integrated into the ranks of professional baseball, just as they had been filtering into the big time prior to the Anson affair. As Holway pointed out in his definitive examination of black stars, *Voices from the Great Black Baseball Leagues*, the "color line" had been broken more than a decade earlier.

As early as 1872 a black man named Bud Fowler became the first Negro to make it in high-class, previously all-white grade-A baseball. In 1884, three years before the Anson incident, brothers Moses and Welday Walker actually played in what then was considered the bigs—Toledo of the American Association. The Walkers were black men.

By the latter part of the 19th century, there were sufficient numbers of high-quality black baseball players in the United States to suggest that if all things were equal—which of course they weren't—dozens of blacks would have been enjoying major league careers by the turn of the century. Even then, black teams such as the Cuban Giants beat the Cincinnati Red

141

Stockings. When the Giants challenged the champion Detroit Tigers in 1887, the Tigers were fortunate to escape with a 6–4 win, taking the game in the ninth on an error.

Because of Cap Anson's ability and his "respectability" in major league baseball, his walkout on George Stovey had the effect of blacklisting all Negro baseball players from the majors. There were, however, a precious few baseball men who were willing to challenge the unwritten law. One of them was John McGraw, who, in 1902, had heard great things about a Negro second baseman and then had the reports confirmed with his own eyes. McGraw was determined to sign Charley Grant for his Baltimore Orioles.

Like George Stovey, Grant was the right man in the wrong place at the wrong time. Although the perceptive McGraw tried to disguise Grant as an Indian, calling him Chief Tokahoma, enough black fans recognized 'the Chief' when the Orioles played in Chicago to inspire White Sox manager Charles Comiskey to do a double take. When Comiskey got wind of McGraw's ploy, it was the end of the white baseball line for Charley Grant.

The blacks finally got the bitter message: they were personae non gratae in major league baseball. The white man owned the bat, the ball, and the stadium. It was as simple as that.

Denied their chance at equal opportunity on the diamond, the blacks did the next best thing; they played among themselves and, whenever possible, scheduled postseason "exhibition" games against white teams. According to records researched by John Holway, of 445 games played between all-white and all-black teams between 1886 and 1948, the whites were defeated, 269–172, with four games ending in a draw. So much for white superiority. (Interestingly, the first all-black World Series in 1903 was held one month *before* the first all-white World Series.)

Not only were the black stars individually excellent, but they frequently outclassed their white counterparts. Thus, Rube Waddell, an outstanding pitcher with the Philadelphia Athletics, was cleanly outpitched by Andrew Foster of the Philadelphia Cuban Giants in the early 1900s.

Likewise, the Detroit Tigers' crack baserunner and batter, Ty Cobb, was so humiliated in 1910 when he was thrown out stealing by the sharp arms of Negro catchers and outhit by three blacks that he refused to play against blacks again. Such accomplishments did not go unnoticed by either the fans or the press. Negro league teams began to draw impressive crowds and black artistry began to inspire even whites to call for official black-white matchups.

One such demand was voiced by the very respected *St. Louis Post-Dispatch.* "There is some doubt," the *Post-Dispatch* proclaimed, "if baseball is, after all, the great American game. We play it, to be sure, but the colored people play it so much better that the time is apparently coming when it shall be known as the great African game."

The *Post-Dispatch* had the likes of Smokey Joe Williams in mind. In 1917, Williams, a black pitcher, went up against the National League pennant winners, the New York Giants. Although he lost, 1–0, on an error, Williams struck out 20 of the champions and didn't allow a single hit.

Meanwhile, Andrew Foster—the very same pitcher who conquered Rube Waddell—had bigger things in mind for his black confreres. At first he nurtured the hope that the 1919–20 Chicago Black Sox scandal would compel white major-league club owners to allow Negroes in the majors. Instead, the whites hired a commissioner, Kenesaw Mountain Landis, who wanted no part of Negroes in the majors.

With this in mind, Foster contacted several black club owners and proposed that they, too, go big time. A conference was called and out of it grew the Negro National League. Year by year the NNL developed a remarkable collection of ball players, most of whom are unknown to the contemporary generation. But in 1927 a stringbean pitcher made his debut for the Birmingham Black Barons, and soon the name of Leroy "Satchel" Paige would become a by-word for quality hurling in the black leagues—and later, in the white American League as well.

What Paige was to black pitching, Josh Gibson was to the Negro catching corps. Those who saw Gibson at his best with the Homestead Greys (playing out of Pittsburgh) rate him the equal or better of Roy Campanella or any other great catcher, past or present, black or white. Gibson's blasts were awesome, and many of Josh's teammates recall them with the same affection one would view his first date or a favorite film. "The longest home run I ever saw Josh hit," remembered Othello Renfroe, who played on some of the best black teams, "was in Shibe Park, Philadelphia. Gibson hit it over everything. Didn't even bounce. Left center. Over the roof—clear over."

Confronting such "outcast" talent presented a problem to the big-league superstars. As artists and athletes, the whites were intrigued by the gifted black players and experienced the normal desire to match their style with the Negroes'. But the sociological factor often intruded—as it did, unfortunately, with

Cap Anson in the 19th century—and many whites simply copped out rather than play with and possibly get beaten by blacks.

THE ST. LOUIS BROWNS NEVER WON A WORLD SERIES, BUT THEY DID WIN A PENNANT IN 1944 AND ALMOST TOOK THE TITLE. WHO DID THEY PLAY, AND HOW CLOSE DID THE BROWNS COME TO WINNING IT ALL?

The Browns' opponents were the St. Louis Cardinals, who were led by Stan Musial, Marty Marion, Whitey Kurowski, and Walker Cooper. The Cards were heavy favorites to win the Series. Every single Cardinals' regular with the exception of second baseman Emil Verban, had tasted World Series competition. Nobody on the Browns had played in a Series, except for manager Luke Sewell and coaches Freddie Hoffman and Zack Taylor. So perhaps, it was suggested, the Browns should throw in the towel.

Probing for some source of optimism, the Browns' high command noted that the Cardinals had suffered a mild slump in September. Was there any meaning to it? Only time would tell—and now the time had come for the first and, as fate would have it, only St. Louis versus St. Louis World Series.

Predictably, St. Louis Cardinals' manager Billy Southworth designated his ace, Morton Cooper (22–7), to deliver the first of the planned one-two-three-four punch to the Browns. Most fans figured that Sewell would counter with either of his two biggest winners, Nelson Potter (19–7) or Jack Kramer (17–13), but Sewell would have nothing of the sort. In a daring move, he held back his aces and picked

32-year-old Denny Galehouse to take on Cooper. Not only had Galehouse never played in a World Series game—he had never *seen* one, and, even more bizarre, he was a relief pitcher. And if that weren't bad enough, Galehouse's record for 1944 was a less-than-imposing 9–10. Nevertheless, Sewell had been impressed with the manner in which Galehouse had pitched in the homestretch, especially in a shutout over the then-contending Yankees. Sewell's dilemma was finding some psychological gimmick with which to instill confidence in his inexperienced ball players. "Gee," said one of the Browns on the eve of the Series opener, "imagine us in a World Series."

The Cardinals were suitably confident. They had finished first in the National League, 14½ games ahead of second-place Pittsburgh, and were designated the "home" team—although the entire Series was to be held at Sportsman's Park—for the first and second Series games as well as the sixth and seventh, if they were needed. If anything, the Cards were overconfident. "Well," cracked Stan Musial, "here we go boys —in another World Series."

Right off the bat, the Cardinals got to Galehouse —almost. Far from sharp, the nervous hurler gave up five hits and a walk in the first three innings and always seemed on the brink of disaster. Yet he bore down in the clutch and managed to escape without giving up a run. Cooper, on the other hand, was breezing past the Browns, and it seemed as if the Redbirds would soon exploit Galehouse's erratic pitching.

In the top of the fourth, Cooper retired the first two batters, but Gene Moore, a former Brooklyn Dodger, singled between first and second. Cooper's next project was George McQuinn, a .250 hitter with 11 home runs to his credit during the regular season.

McQuinn responded with a lavish drive over the right-field seats. Those were all the hits the Browns would obtain for the rest of the game.

Galehouse responded to McQuinn's howitzer with an offensive of his own, and the Cards went scoreless in the fourth, fifth, sixth, seventh, and eighth innings. Kurowski singled for the Redbirds in the eighth, but it hardly was cause for concern in the Browns' dugout, since Galehouse snuffed out the budding rally and only would have to face the bottom of the Cardinals' batting order in the last of the ninth.

Slats Marion led off the Cardinals' ninth with a drive to center that bounced off Mike Kreevich's glove for a double. When Augie Burgamo grounded out, second to first, Marion raced to third. At this point, manager Billy Southworth sent Ken O'Dea up to pinch-hit for relief pitcher Blix Donnelly. O'Dea's fly to center was deep enough to score the Cardinals' first run. It was now a 2–1 game, Browns.

Speedy Johnny Hopp now stood between Galehouse and the Browns' first World Series victory. Would Galehouse hang tough? Would he crack? A minute later, the Sportsman's Park enthusiasts had the answer as they hailed Galehouse, who had induced Hopp to fly out harmlessly. The Browns suddenly had been converted from buffoons to the behemoths of the 1944 Series.

Manager Sewell's ploy had worked so well that pundits wondered whether he would try another stunner to start game two. But this time the Browns followed a traditional course and named Nelson Potter, their ace of aces during the regular season, to start the match, while Southworth selected Max Lanier (17–12). In the press room before the game, there were those who theorized that the Cards had been caught

147

napping in the opener and would respond with a vengeance in game two. The Browns, they suggested, had made the mistake of awakening the Cardinal giant.

As a Cardinal-killer, Potter was no Galehouse—the Redbirds got to him in the third inning. After Verban singled, Potter could have avoided any further trouble if he had firmly grasped Lanier's pop-up bunt, but he dropped the attempted sacrifice and then, in a fit of pique, pegged the ball wildly past first for a double error, allowing Verban to reach third, from where he scored on an infield out. The Browns, who had played errorless ball in the opener, continued to treat the horsehide as if it were covered with grease. Third baseman Mark Christman bobbled a grounder in the fourth that led to another Cardinal run.

True, the Cardinals owned a 2–0 lead, but they hardly appeared overpowering in the field or at the plate. Manager Sewell's concern was his impotent batsmen, who did nothing for five innings. However, in the top of the sixth, Moore singled, Red Hayworth doubled, and Frank Mancuso, pinch-hitting for Potter, came through with another single and—*smash-bam alakazam!*—the Browns had tied the game. Better still, Sewell invited Bob Muncrief (13–8) in from the bullpen for a fresh, solid arm, while Southworth stayed with Lanier. Neither team scored in the seventh, but the Browns threatened to take the lead when Kreevich led off the eighth with a convincing double. It was enough to persuade Southworth to give Lanier the hook and in from the bullpen came the ubiquitous Blix Donnelly for the second time in two days.

The little right-hander with the confusing curveball encountered the meat of the Browns' batting order—Chet Laabs and Vern Stephens, in sequence.

First, Laabs went down swinging, then Stephens followed suit. Ray Sanders received an intentional walk, but Mark Christman blew the Browns' chances by striking out, too. No slouch himself, Muncrief kept the Cards at bay through the bottom of the ninth and the game went into extra innings.

It was now apparent to the 35,076 witnesses that the St. Louis Browns were fluke pennant winners no longer. They may not have had the Cards' power, but they scratched and somehow managed to stay in the ball game. And with extra innings on tap, who knows —they might even make it two in a row over the Cardinals.

Neither team scored in the tenth, but the Browns made a bold bid in the top of the 11th. McQuinn, a magnificent figure for the underdogs, started the inning with a double. Christman was next to bat, and Sewell ordered a rudimentary sacrifice bunt to push McQuinn over to third. Christman obliged, but Donnelly, in an astonishing example of anticipation, pounced on the ball and fired to third baseman Kurowski, who tagged out the onrushing McQuinn. With tragic irony for the Browns, Gene Moore followed with a long fly to Musial in right that would have been the perfect sacrifice. For the Browns, once again it was close, but no cigar. They itched to get another shot at Donnelly in the 12th inning.

But to do so they would have to stifle the Cardinals in the bottom of the 11th, and the home club had different ideas. First, Sanders tagged Muncrief for a single, then Kurowski sacrificed him to second. Marion received an intentional walk, whereupon Southworth made another decisive move. Instead of allowing Verban to bat, the manager waved Ken O'Dea to the plate as pinch hitter. "I wanna get home to dinner," snapped O'Dea, as he strode to the batter's box—then banged Muncrief's second pitch safely to right. The Cardinals had won the marathon, 3–2. Each team had collected seven hits, but the Browns were guilty of four errors, the Cards none.

With the Series tied at one game apiece, there was good news and bad news for the Browns as they approached the third match. The good news was that Sewell's athletes would be the "home" team for a change. The bad news was the weather. It was a broiling 90-degree-plus day on October 6, 1944, and Browns' starter Jack Kramer was livid. Winner of 17 games, loser of 13, Kramer beefed, "I hate the hot weather. But if the boys just get a few hits and a few runs for me, I'll be all right."

The heat seemed to get to Kramer right at the start. With Hopp on second (thanks, in part to Stephens's error), Kramer gave up a single to Walker Cooper, and the Cardinals had the first run of the game. Already Sewell was worried. When Kramer walked Sanders, Sewell ordered Al Hollingsworth, a gray-haired journeyman pitcher who had worn the uniforms of five different clubs, to start throwing in the bullpen. Whitey Kurowski, who wielded a terrifying bat, was up next, and Browns' fans expected the worst. But Kramer managed to find himself and send the crack third baseman back to the dugout with a strikeout.

Armed with a run, Ted Wilks, who had completed a tidy 17–4 record during the season, took the mound against the Browns. All was well with Wilks until the second inning, when, unexpectedly, he loaded the bases with three walks. Lucky for Wilks, Kramer was the next batter, and, with two outs, he conveniently whiffed, thereby ending the inning.

Nevertheless, the near-rally for the Browns did absolutely no good for Wilks's ulcer. One inning later he was out of the box.

The Browns' assault—their biggest of the Series—began with singles by Moore, Stephens, McQuinn, Al Zarilla, and Christman. Southworth yanked Wilks and replaced him with Fred Schmidt, who complicated matters with an intentional pass and a wild pitch. The Cardinals were playing—or misplaying—the way the Browns were supposed to, and they allowed four fat runs. "That's what I wanted," said Kramer as he took the mound in the top of the fourth.

Kramer manacled the Cardinals' batters the way teammate Denny Galehouse had done in the opening game. One by one they hit mildly or not at all, while the Browns collected two more runs on doubles by Stephens and McQuinn and a Walker Cooper passed ball in the seventh inning. The final score was 6–2, Browns, and now they had a two-game-to-one lead, not to mention an enormous psychological edge. If somehow they could make more magic, the greatest miracle in baseball history would come to pass—the St. Louis Browns would win the World Series.

Asked to continue the streak was Sig Jakucki, the pitching hero of the season's finale that won the Browns the pennant. The Browns made a valiant effort, but they were foiled by sensational Cardinal fielding. Jakucki couldn't contain the Cards' big hitters and the Browns lost, 5–1.

In the fifth game the Brownies got brilliant pitching from Denny Galehouse, but his teammates failed to score and so the Cards won, 2–0.

The Browns' final hope was Nelson Potter, who had a 1–0 lead going into the fourth inning of game six. In the fourth the Cards put runners on first and third with one out. Whitey Kurowski then hit a grounder to Vern Stephens that appeared to be a sure double play. Stephens tossed it to Don Gutteridge at second, who fired to McQuinn at first for what appeared to be an inning-ending twin killing. But the umpires ruled that Gutteridge had failed to touch second. The suddenly alive Cardinals accumulated three runs, which was all they needed to win the game, 3–1, and the World Series.

If nothing else, the Brownies earned the everlasting respect of the Cards. As Cardinal shortstop and the major league Player of the Year Marty Marion put it, "We thought we were going to just walk through them. Who in hell's the Browns, you know. By the time we got in that first game, we found out they were a pretty good ball club. Yes, sir, we had a hell of a time beating those boys. They were tough. If they'd have beat us that second game we'd have probably been in trouble. We had a good ball club but it wasn't great. They had quite a bit of pride.

"That Streetcar Series. If the Browns had beat us, that would have been really a disgrace."

CHARLIE FINLEY FEUDED WITH INNUMERABLE PLAYERS AND OWNERS DURING HIS TEMPESTUOUS REIGN AS ONE OF THE LORDS OF BASEBALL. FEW OF HIS BATTLES MATCHED HIS DISPUTES WITH ACE PITCHER VIDA BLUE. CAN YOU CITE ANY OF THE REASONS BEHIND THEIR DISPUTES?

The roots of their antagonism were planted when Charlie wanted Blue to change his first name to "True." Vida had been named for his father and was proud to bear the name. "If Finley likes that name so much," bellowed Blue, "why doesn't he change his name?"

In 1971, Finley was paying Blue $14,750, a mere half-step above the major-league minimum salary, when the left-hander from Mansfield, Louisiana, got off to a sensational start on his way to a sterling 24–8 campaign. Reasonable pundits suggested that Finley should tear up Blue's contract during the season and give Vida a hefty increase. Such was not the case with Charlie O., who, in place of dollars, presented his new ace with a Cadillac bearing the license plate "BLUE" and credit cards for gas. Blue was furious; he did not want to project what he regarded as the negative image of a black driving a Cadillac. What grated Blue the most was the unmistakable suggestion that Finley had, in his own perverse way, patted Blue on the head and told him that since he had been such a good boy, he had won himself a present. "Why didn't he just tear up my contract and give me a new one?" inquired Blue. "He got back in publicity alone more than the Cadillac ever cost him."

The following spring, Blue, on the recommendation of his roommate Tommy Davis, hired attorney Robert J. Gerst and ordered the lawyer to get the money he believed he was worth from Finley. The contract talks should have been featured in a burlesque theater. Blue asked for a minimum salary of $115,000, while Finley's best offer was $50,000.

Enter Baseball Commissioner Bowie Kuhn, and the serious hammering out of an agreement began. Ultimately a contract was agreed upon. Finley, of course, was unhappy because Blue was going to receive much more than $50,000. Besides that, Charlie felt Blue was in poor physical shape, having missed

153

training camp, and even after he did work himself into shape, Blue never regained the form he had displayed the previous year. As a result, Blue's drawing power suffered terribly and the A's attendance fell below the one million mark.

Blue interestingly defined the difference between his style and Finley's: "There is confidence and there is cocky confidence," Blue said. "I have confidence. Charlie Finley has cocky confidence."

Blue never forgave Finley for his condescending treatment during the contract dispute—like a "damned colored boy" is the way Blue described it. Riveted in Vida's mind was Finley's manner of quoting Blue with a subtly derogatory, slight southern accent—which, by the way, Blue does not have. Finley would inject "soulisms" such as "pacific" instead of "specific."

"Vida," Charlie O concluded, "is basically a good boy."

"Charlie Finley," said Vida Blue, "has soured my stomach for baseball."

BELIEVE IT OR NOT, SIX MISPLAYS ONCE WERE COMMITTED ON A SINGLE PLAY IN A WORLD SERIES GAME. WHO WERE THE CULPRITS?

The madcap merry-go-round of miscues developed in the second game of the 1944 World Series between the St. Louis Browns and the St. Louis Cardinals. In the Cardinals' half of the third inning, Emil Verban opened with a single. The next batter, pitcher Max Lanier, attempted a sacrifice bunt and popped the ball up in the infield. Now all hell broke loose among the Browns' infielders.

Brownies manager Luke Sewell recalled the incident to author William B. Mead in the book *Even the Browns*. "We made six misplays on the ball. That's pretty difficult. He popped a little ball down the third-base line. Potter and Christman came over to it. They looked at each other and let the ball drop, and Potter picked it up and he rolled it up his arm. That's two misplays.

"He threw it to Gutteridge at first. Little Don was trying to hold his foot on the bag and get the ball, when he should have gotten off and caught the ball. It went down into right field. That's three.

"Chet Laabs let it hit that right-field wall there, reached over to pick it up, and it rolled through his legs. That's four. He picked the ball up and fumbled on his pickup—that's five—and threw it away at second base. That's six misplays on the one ball."

Technically, two errors were charged on the play, both to the Browns' pitcher. As far as Sewell was concerned, it was a six-error blunder, and one he'll never forget.

HAS ANY TEAM EVER COME FROM BEHIND TO WIN THE WORLD SERIES IN THE BOTTOM OF THE LAST INNING OF THE SEVENTH GAME?

Yes, it happened once. In 1912 the Boston Red Sox scored twice in the bottom of the 10th inning to defeat the New York Giants, 3–2, and win the World Series, four games to three.

Note: there had been one tie during the 1912 tournament, and the final game was actually the eighth of the Series.

THE 1972 WORLD CHAMPION OAKLAND
ATHLETICS HAD THREE PITCHERS WITH
THE SAME EARNED RUN AVERAGE OF 2.51.
WHO WERE THEY?

Rollie Fingers, Ken Holtzman, and John "Blue
Moon" Odom.

BASEBALL LEGEND HAS IT THAT THE
TEAM IN FIRST PLACE ON THE FOURTH OF
JULY WILL WIN THE PENNANT. OF THE
44 DIVISION WINNERS DURING THE YEARS
1969–1979, HOW MANY OF THEM CELE-
BRATED INDEPENDENCE DAY IN FIRST
PLACE?

A total of 27.

The National League West, with eight, had the
most. Both American League divisions had seven,
and the National League East had six. Five times the
American League West's Oakland A's were in first
place on July 4, and five times they won their division.
The Cincinnati Reds and Baltimore Orioles are second in that category.

There were 17 pennant winners in that bunch.
All seven American League East teams went on to
win their league championship. Six of those 17 were
in the National League West, and three in the American League West. Only one was in the National
League East. Eight of those teams won the World
Series.

FOUR AMERICAN LEAGUE TEAMS HOLD THE MAJOR LEAGUE RECORD OF LEAVING 15 MEN ON BASE DURING A GAME IN WHICH THEY WERE SHUT OUT. NAME AT LEAST TWO OF THE CLUBS.

The New York Yankees, on May 22, 1913, against the St. Louis Browns; the Washington Senators, on July 29, 1931, against the Indians; the Browns, on August 1, 1941, against the Yankees; and the Kansas City Royals, on May 12, 1975, against the Detroit Tigers.

DURING THE 1980 SEASON A MONTREAL EXPOS' PITCHER SET THE MAJOR LEAGUE RECORD FOR MOST STRIKEOUTS BY A ROOKIE PITCHER IN A NINE-INNING GAME. WHO IS HE?

Bill Gullickson, who was 21 years old at the time, struck out 18 Chicago Cubs on the night of September 10, 1980. He broke the record of 15, which had been held by J. R. Richard of Houston and Karl Spooner of the Brooklyn Dodgers.

Interestingly, while warming up that night, Gullickson felt insecure. "When I warmed up," he said after the game, "my arm felt tight and I didn't feel like I had my good stuff." Gullickson also said that he "just blanked the record out of my mind because I'm not really a strikeout pitcher."

But he certainly was that night. Not only did he set the rookie mark, but only three pitchers—Nolan Ryan, Tom Seaver, and Steve Carlton, each of whom fanned 19—had ever struck out more men in one game. And Gullickson's 18 were the most in the majors since Ron Guidry whiffed 18 California Angels in 1978.

THE 1967 ALL-STAR GAME WAS WON BY THE NATIONAL LEAGUE, 2–1. ALL THREE OF THE GAME'S RUNS WERE SCORED ON HOME RUNS, BY THREE DIFFERENT THIRD BASEMEN. CAN YOU NAME ANY OF THE TRIO?

Richie Allen of Philadelphia homered off Minnesota's Dean Chance in the second inning to give the Nationals a 1–0 lead. In the sixth, Baltimore Oriole third baseman Brooks Robinson smashed a round-tripper off Chicago Cub hurler Ferguson Jenkins, allowing the Junior Circuit to tie the game at 1–1.

A full nine innings later, in the top of the 15th inning, Cincinnati's Tony Perez hit a Catfish Hunter pitch out of the stadium to give the National League its victory. (Although he's better known as a first basemen, Perez also was a fine third baseman much of the early part of his career.)

TED WILLIAMS WAS ONE OF THE GREATEST HITTERS OF ALL TIME AND SHOULD HAVE BEEN ONE OF THE MOST POPULAR PLAYERS ON THE BOSTON RED SOX. BUT IN HIS ROOKIE SEASON AN EPISODE TOOK PLACE THAT PERMANENTLY ANGERED BEANTOWN FANS AND ALTERED WILLIAMS'S IMAGE FOREVER. WHAT WAS IT?

According to Al Hirshberg, the late Boston journalist and Red Sox historian, Williams appeared to be a guaranteed hit with the Boston fans when he arrived at Fenway Park from San Diego. But only a short time elapsed before Williams had become a problem for the Boston media and the fans.

The cold war between Williams and the media was exacerbated by the preferential treatment the slugger received from his boss, owner Tom Yawkey. "Ted," said Hirshberg, "saw fit to treat the Boston press—with two notable exceptions—as human beings in the spring and dogs from Memorial Day on. In common with many of my colleagues, I found Williams the most aggravating and most interesting personality in baseball."

There were no signs of a conflict in 1939, when Williams arrived in Beantown as a rather joyful 20-year-old who stood 6'-3" and could poke the ball a country mile. There was, however, a fatal flaw in Williams' armor: he betrayed an awkward gait that made him appear to be moving slower than he actually was. Even when Williams labored vigorously, he appeared to be loafing. Ted's first brush with the fans developed as a result of a misplayed grounder in his freshman year. In the middle of the 1939 season, Williams was in right field when a ground ball trickled through his legs. "When he turned to chase it," said Hirshberg, "his awkward gallop made it appear that he wasn't running as fast as he could."

When Ted arrived at the right-field fence, he was stunned by a wave of boos. Instead of leaving bad-enough alone, Williams cursed the fans, and a lifetime war had begun. Minutes later, Ted confirmed the outbreak of hostilities by telling his teammates in the dugout, "Those sonsofabitches! I'll never tip my cap to them again!"

Williams was true to his word. Unfortunately, his honesty turned out to be hardly diplomatic, and before he ever had a chance to revise his strategy—not that he ever planned to—two pivotal pillars of the press had turned on him: Austen "Duke" Lake of the Boston *American* and Dave Egan of the *Record-American*. Sandwiched between their big verbal cannons, Williams figured he never had a chance. They withered Ted in print within a week of the episode and maintained a steady barrage of vitriol for years afterward. "That," Hirshberg explained, "completed Williams's disenchantment with Boston, its fans, and its press."

To protect himself against the assaults, Williams invoked several personal acts of defiance. He refused to speak to Egan and Lake and soon had decided upon a verbal embargo against most of the other Boston writers. Once, when the Red Sox had voted to ban the press for an entire hour after the game, newsmen squirmed outside the clubhouse as the minutes ticked off. Finally, the locker-room door was opened, by Williams of all people, and the slugger snapped at the reporters, "Okay, now all you bastards can come in!" Williams was the only member of the Red Sox left in the clubhouse.

While some hypersensitive athletes might have allowed their off-the-field feuds to interfere with their on-the-field performance, Williams managed to blunt the spades before they affected his bat. The kid they came to call the Splendid Splinter batted .327 in 1939 and showed promise that without equivocation, in time, he just might be the best batter in history.

Egan and Lake were unimpressed. "They blasted Williams regularly," Hirshberg once recalled. "They rarely found anything good to say about his play.

They even criticized his superb hitting on the grounds that it usually came at times when it helped the ball club least and Williams most."

Although few were as steadfastly anti-Williams in their prose, a sizable number of reporters seemed to delight in Egan's and Lake's endless crusade. The pair reflected their hostility toward Ted by denying him (by voting for someone else) at least two Most Valuable Player awards. As for the fans, they didn't have the official voting power, but they did have lungs and used them whenever and wherever possible against Williams. "Ted's basic offense against the fans," said writer and baseball fan John Updike, "was to wish that they weren't there."

The other obvious way to shut everybody up was with a swing of his bat. In 1940 Ted lifted his average to .344, and in 1941 he whacked the ball (and presumably his foes) to the tune of a .406 mark. Ted then bade Boston goodbye and served for three years as a Marine pilot.

Williams returned from the war but hardly found peace in quaint Beantown. He resumed his battles with the press as if he had only been gone a few days. One of Ted's most consistent—and irritating to the regular reporters—ploys was to feed scoops to Johnny Garro, sports editor of Boston's Italian-language paper, *La Notizia*. Sometimes days would go by before the regulars realized they were being scooped by a tiny Italian paper.

If Williams' attitude had been unchanged by World War II, neither had his performance at the plate. He hit a mighty .342 in 1946 and the Red Sox, to the astonishment of some, virtually annexed the American League pennant by midsummer. At the end of July they were in first place, 12 games ahead of the hated Yankees. Williams was superb—he had led the American League to a 12–0 rout over the Nationals in the All-Star Game in Boston, with two homers and two singles—and was abetted by a formidable Red Sox pitching staff. Boston won the pennant, although they staggered through September as if the entire club would disintegrate. And then in the Series, leading the St. Louis Cardinals three games to two, Boston blew the next two games and the championship.

To say that Williams failed in his first (and only) World Series would be an understatement. He batted only .200, whereas had he been the Williams of less tension-filled moments, he could very well have won the Series for Boston. "It has always been Williams's records first, the team second," Boston *American* columnist Huck Finnegan was to write, "and the Sox non-winning record is proof enough of that."

Ted had ample opportunity to redeem himself in 1948 at a time when the Red Sox rightfully bragged that they had one of the best teams that ever graced a diamond. Pitching, which always had been the club's Achilles' heel, was bolstered by a deal with the St. Louis Browns in which in exchange for three substitutes and $65,000 cash, the Red Sox obtained right-hander Ellis Kinder and infielder Billy Hitchcock. A day later, the Bostons delivered seven more mediocrities as well as $310,000 to the Browns, and this time received right-hander Jack Kramer and hard-hitting shortstop Vernon "Junior" Stephens. As an added fillip, the Sox had as their manager "Marse" Joe McCarthy, who had been a legend in New York, managing numerous Yankee champion championship clubs.

Until McCarthy appeared on the Beantown scene, Williams had established, among other idiosyncrasies, that he would not wear a necktie if he could help it. McCarthy, on the other hand, had always insisted that his Yankees display sartorial splendor. The Bronx Bombers wore neckties, or else. A head-on collision seemed inevitable when the Red Sox reported for spring training at the Saratoga Terrace Hotel. What, everyone wondered, would McCarthy do with his brooding superstar?

Marse Joe executed a magnificent strategy—he appeared at breakfast in the coffee shop of the hotel without a necktie and with his shirt open at the collar. "From that day on," wrote Hirshberg, "Williams thought he was the best manager who ever lived. So did others who saw the incident."

Under McCarthy in 1948, the Red Sox started the season like a collection of clods—they were 11½ games out of first place by Memorial Day—but rallied to take over first by August 23. Williams was en route to a hefty .369 batting average and, one would have imagined, such a talented lineup would cruise easily to the pennant. Unfortunately for proper and improper Bostonians alike, both the Cleveland Indians and the New York Yankees were prepared to argue the point.

Neither the Yankees nor the Indians showed any inclination to wilt as the three teams circled into the homestretch. A Red Sox pennant loomed as a particularly enthralling prospect to New Englanders because the Boston Braves had already clinched the National League flag. A Subway Series was in the offing—with a little help from Williams.

On the next-to-last day of the season, the Red Sox did come through, whipping the Yankees and thereby eliminating them from contention. Yet they were still a game behind Cleveland and faced the Yanks once more. Boston won again—while Cleveland lost to Detroit—and finished in a dead heat with the Indians. First place would be ultimately decided in a one-game playoff at friendly Fenway Park.

Williams was as far from being the hero of the play-off as British Columbia is from Boston Common. Player-manager Lou Boudreau of the Indians had a perfect day at the plate with two homers, two singles, and a walk in five at bats. "Williams flopped," wrote Finnegan. The Red Sox were knocked out of the pennant box in an 8–3 rout.

Williams's failure no longer provided fodder for Lake and Egan alone. "Ted," said Hirshberg, "had become everybody's favorite target. Soon the newcomers among the press began to find flaws in other ball players, too. . . . The press in other cities, particularly Cleveland and Detroit, was fully as vitriolic, but no other city had a Ted Williams. Because of his prominence, he was the reason for Boston's reputation as a tough newspaper town."

Not that everybody who covered baseball for a living stuck pins in a Williams doll. There were those, such as the eminent John Updike, who raised the Splendid Splinter to the very highest pedestal, warts and all. "It may be," wrote Updike, "that compared to managers' dreams such as Joe DiMaggio and the always helpful Stan Musial, Williams was an icy star. But of all team sports, baseball, with its graceful intermittences of action, its immense and tranquil field sparsely settled with men in white, its dispassionate mathematics, seems to me best suited to accommodate, and be ornamented by a loner."

THE FIRST HINTS THAT THE CHICAGO WHITE SOX WERE DUMPING THE 1919 WORLD SERIES TO THE CINCINNATI REDS IN THE INFAMOUS "BLACK SOX" SCANDAL CAME DURING THE FIRST TWO GAMES OF THE SERIES. DO YOU KNOW WHAT HINTS LED TO THESE SUSPICIONS?

Evidence that all was not right with the World Series became apparent on October 1, 1919, after more than 30,000 fans had filled the Reds' stadium to see the opener of the Fall Classic. Dutch Reuther was on the mound for the home club as Shano Collins led off for Chicago. He promptly stung the partisan audience with a sharp single to center, bringing White Sox captain Eddie Collins to the plate.

Eddie Collins botched a simple sacrifice bunt, forcing Shano Collins at second. Already Eddie Collins, a Sox player who had nothing to do with the fix, was accidentally contributing to his team's demise. Collins, trying to compensate for his bad bunt, then tried to steal second and was thrown out with ease. The White Sox went out of the first inning without a run.

Now it was the Reds' half of the inning and the time for the prime "fixer," Ed Cicotte, to take the mound and do his stuff, as perfectly as possible. This would have been a simpler matter if his catcher had been involved in the fix, but the veteran Ray Schalk was in the Collins camp, and Cicotte would have to do without Schalk's aid.

Among the pregame rumors was one that Ed Cicotte's arm was sore and sure enough, he looked bad, hitting the Reds' leadoff batter, Morris Rath, in the back. Cicotte was earning his "fix." After one inning the Reds led, 1–0. But Chicago tied the score

165

in the top of the second and the clubs remained dead-locked until the bottom of the fourth.

Although he had allowed but a single run and apparently had the Reds in hand, Cicotte was a tired man as he prepared for the first batter in the fourth, Edd Roush. Catcher Ray Schalk, an intense competitor, had been displeased with his pitcher's languorous behavior. Still, a 1–1 tie on enemy turf was nothing to complain about. Cicotte began deliberately to slip, a bum pitch here and a foolish pause in fielding a ball there. Still, he couldn't ruin it completely and the Reds only had a man on first with two out. But the next batter punched a grounder through the middle, putting runners on first and second and Ivy Wingo up to bat. Cicotte pitched, and Wingo singled home Larry Kopf. Dutch Reuther, the next batter, figured to be an easy third out. Instead, the Reds' pitcher belted a towering triple, scoring two more runs. Morris Rath followed with another hit and now it was turning into a runaway, especially after Jack Daubert also came through with a hit and the Reds led, 6–1. Manager Kid Gleason had had enough; he yanked Cicotte, replacing him with Roy Wilkinson. It was, however, an exercise in futility since all the necessary damage had been done. The Reds scored three more times and wrapped up the opener, 9–1.

The overwhelming defeat of the White Sox had confirmed almost everyone's fears within the club's inner circle. Manager Kid Gleason had heard the rumors and so had owner Charles Comiskey. By the afternoon of October 2, there would be more evidence with which to judge the events—and rumors. It was time for the second game, with Lefty Williams due to pitch for Chicago.

Baseball's popularity had grown so rapidly since the end of World War I that the big-league entrepreneurs had decided to lengthen the World Series from a best-of-seven to a best-of-nine tournament. This meant that the White Sox one-game deficit was hardly worth worrying about—if Kid Gleason's players were to play up to their potential. For the second go-around, the Sox would face Harry "Slim" Sallee, a 35-year-old who had won 21 games and lost only seven during the regular season. Manager Pat Moran of Cincinnati was more than pleased with the Cardinal and Giant discard. On a good day Slim could more than compensate for the Reds' relatively weak hitting, and he showed his stuff was sharp in the top of the first inning as the crowd hailed another runless frame for the visitors from Chicago.

With Lefty Williams on the mound, the Reds looked feeble, going out in order, one-two-three. The White Sox did likewise and when Williams returned for the second inning, he mowed the Reds down like a champion. Nobody, on the available evidence, could accuse him of dumping—at least, not yet. Ironically the White Sox were belting the ball now, but they suffered incredibly bad luck—Schalk just missed hitting a home run onto the left-field roof—and for three innings the game remained scoreless.

Chicago's big bats failed to explode in the top of the fourth, and Morris Rath launched the Cincinnati effort in the last half of the inning with a walk. Jake Daubert wasted no time laying down a sacrifice bunt, sending Rath to second. These were the exploitative Reds at their best. Next came Heinie Groh, who, like Rath, walked on a three-and-two count. Williams had reached the meat of the home club's batting order:

their bread-and-butter batter, Edd Roush. Just as the audience had hoped, Roush produced a hit, scoring Rath and moving Groh to third.

Fortunately for Gleason and the Chicago supporters, there still were some worthies on the White Sox club, among them catcher Schalk. When Roush tried to steal second, the diminutive catcher pegged him out as if he had a heat missile attached to his arm. But Williams wasn't cooperating; pitching wildly, he walked Pat Duncan. Cincinnati revved up its rally when Kopf poked a terrific triple to left.

With three runs in the fourth and another in the sixth, the Reds entered the final phase of the game with a fair but not insurmountable lead. The White Sox WERE hitting; they outhit their foe, 10–4, for the game and managed two runs in the top of the seventh. But that was it for Gleason's troops; they lost the second match, 4–2.

A PLAYER WHO ACTUALLY WAS MISSING A LEG WORE THE UNIFORM OF A BIG-LEAGUE TEAM. CAN YOU NAME THE INDIVIDUAL AND THE TEAM?

Bert Shepard was a pilot in the Army Air Corps during World War II when his plane was shot down. Captured by the Nazis, Shepard was taken to a prisoner-of-war hospital, where his leg was amputated between the knee and the ankle. One of Shepard's buddies fashioned an artificial leg for Bert and eventually he returned to the United States as part of a prisoner-exchange deal with the Germans. It was 1945 and the war was still on when the U.S. War Department asked Shepard to tour the 1945 spring training camps of the Washington Senators and New York Yankees as a morale booster.

Shepard agreed and while at the Senators' camp, he suggested to Manager Ossie Bluege that he might be good enough to pitch for Washington. The tryout was successful, and Bert performed admirably in an exhibition game against the Norfolk Naval Training Station team. Nevertheless, manager Bluege was convinced that Shepard would not be able to handle a regular big-league workload and signed Bert as a coach. He did, however, make one regular appearance in relief and pitched well for five innings, allowing three hits and one run. He also pitched in an exhibition game and beat the Brooklyn Dodgers.

SEVERAL MAJOR LEAGUERS WERE KILLED OR WOUNDED WHILE SERVING IN THE ARMED FORCES DURING WORLD WAR II. CAN YOU NAME ANY OF THEM?

One of the best players of all before the war was Cecil Travis of the Washington Senators. A combatant during the hellish Battle of the Bulge (Belgium, 1944–45), Travis came out of the assault with badly frozen feet. When he returned to the Senators at the conclusion of the war he was unable to regain his prewar abilities.

Another former Senators player, Elmer Gedeon, died in action, as did Harry O'Neill, who played but one game for the Philadelphia Athletics. Ironically, Billy Southworth, Jr., son of the St. Louis Cardinals manager, survived 25 bombing missions over Europe but died trying to make an emergency landing at

LaGuardia Field in Queens, New York, in February 1945.

Among other prospects who suffered as a result of the war were Johnny Grodzicki of the St. Louis Cardinals, who was considered a potential 20-game winner. Because of a wound, Grodzicki was unable to use his right leg effectively and was only a shade of his former prewar self. Likewise, Cardinal infielder Frank "Creepy" Crespi lost his chance at a postwar career because of a pair of weird mishaps. First, Crespi broke his leg during an army baseball game. Then, while recovering, he participated in a wheelchair race at his hospital and rebroke the leg.

Few suffered as terribly as Philadelphia Athletics' pitcher Lou Brissie, a soldier in the Italian campaign. Wounded by shell fragments, Brissie was hospitalized with two broken feet, a crushed left ankle, and a broken left leg, as well as injuries to his hands and shoulders. Brissie not only recovered from his wounds but joined the Athletics after the war and developed into a first-rate pitcher.

Still another hero was pitcher Phil Marchildon of the Athletics, an airman whose plane was shot down by the Nazis. Taken to a prisoner-of-war camp, Marchildon lost 30 pounds over a period of a year but survived. When he returned to the United States, his physical condition was so precarious that many doubted he would pitch again. However, the Athletics' manager Connie Mack persuaded Marchildon into putting on a uniform for a Phil Marchildon Night. More than 30,000 Philadelphians turned out to cheer Phil, who responded by pitching three innings. A year later he was pitching like the Marchildon of old, winning 13 and losing 16 for the Athletics. His best season was 1947, when he went 19–9.

THE 1944 WORLD SERIES BETWEEN THE
ST. LOUIS CARDINALS AND THE ST. LOUIS
BROWNS PROVED AN EMBARRASSMENT FOR
THE WIVES OF THE RIVAL MANAGERS, BILLY
SOUTHWORTH AND LUKE SEWELL. WHY?

Actually, Sewell and Southworth were on good
terms; so good, in fact, that they had an arrangement
whereby their respective families shared the same
apartment in St. Louis. This was possible during the
regular season, since the Browns and Cardinals never
were in the city simultaneously. When the Browns
(and Luke Sewell) would go on the road, Mrs. Sewell
would head for Akron, Ohio, where her family lived.

Each family kept its belongings at different ends
of the apartment and the arrangement worked out
harmoniously until both the Cardinals and the Browns
won their respective pennants. With both teams
camped in St. Louis for the World Series, a problem
arose over tenancy of the Lindell Towers apartment
shared by the Southworths and Sewells.

"It would never do," wrote William B. Mead,
author of *Even The Browns*, "for the opposing managers to sit in the same living room after a World
Series game, sipping bourbon and chatting politely
with their wives. Sewell wanted to invite his mother,
and Mrs. Southworth could hardly be expected to
put up with a mother-in-law from the wrong family
and, indeed, the wrong league."

The dilemma was resolved when it was learned
that another tenant in the building was leaving town
for the duration of the World Series. He graciously
agreed to allow the Southworths to camp in his abode
until the Series was over.

Sewell immediately invited his mother to St.
Louis from her home in Alabama. Mrs. Sewell had

never seen a big-league ball game in her life, and her proud son was certain that she would be tickled to see him manage in the World Series. Mrs. Sewell arrived in time to see Luke's Browns win the opener, 2-1. Mrs. Sewell also showed up at Sportsman's Park for game two, only this time the Browns lost a heartbreaker, 3-2, in 11 innings.

The Browns' manager recalled with a mixture of bitterness and wry amusement his mother's reaction. "After the second game, I must have stayed up in the clubhouse an hour and a half. Finally I got out and went to the apartment. My mother liked a rocking chair. Well, I had a rocking chair for her and she was rocking away. I went up, put my arm around her shoulder, and I said, 'Mom, what did you think of that game today?' They had beat us in 11 innings, you know. 'Oh,' she said, 'I was awfully glad when someone won because I was getting mighty tired.'

"It just about broke my heart."

A ONE-ARMED OUTFIELDER AND A DEAF OUTFIELDER PLAYED BOTH MAJOR AND MINOR LEAGUE BASEBALL AT THE SAME TIME. WHO WERE THEY?

The deaf player was Dick Sipek and the one-armed pro was Pete Gray.

During World War II, Gray emerged as a star with Memphis of the Class A Southern Association while Sipek did very well for Birmingham in the same circuit. Gray captured nationwide attention in 1944 when he hit .333 and stole 63 bases for Memphis. Equally amazing was his ability in the field—he led the Southern Association in fielding percentage. To do so, Gray had to surmount the obvious problem of fielding the ball with one arm, then disposing of the glove and firing the horsehide back to the infield. Baseball historian William B. Mead described Gray's deft execution of the maneuver as follows: "Removing almost all the padding from his glove, Gray wore it on his fingertips with his little finger out. He would catch the ball, stick his glove under the stump of his right arm, draw the ball clear with his left hand, and throw it to the infield."

Sipek played against Gray in the Southern Association in 1943 and 1944. What hearing defects he may have had were not sufficient to overshadow his ability. He batted well over .300 and used his eyes to make up for his hearing deficiencies.

"Wherever he played," Mead reported, "Sipek trained the center fielder and the second and first baseman to let him decide who was to catch a batted ball. If Sipek called for it, they had to get out of the way, because he could not hear their calls. If he did not call for it, it was their's to catch."

Both Gray and Sipek graduated to the majors in 1945, Sipek with the Cincinnati Reds and Gray with the St. Louis Browns. The deaf outfielder played in 31 games for the Reds and batted .244. Some of Sipek's teammates learned sign language, including the signs for profanity. When Dick once was called out on a close play, his hands angrily cursed the umpire in sign language. The arbiter did not realize the depth of the profanity, but some of Sipek's teammates did and roared their approval. A year later Sipek was in the minors to stay.

Gray's one year in the bigs had its high and its low points. Several critics believed that Pete was there more as a publicity stunt than anything else. Yet he managed to hit .218 over 61 games and stole five bases. The Browns, who had won the American League pennant in 1944, were believed to be contenders in 1945, but many critics argued that Gray cost them first place. "Pete did great with what he had," said teammate Mark Christman. "But he cost us the pennant in 1945. We finished third, only six games out."

A year later, Gray was playing for Toledo. He never wore a major league uniform again.

The Quickie Quiz

1. The first relief pitcher to win a Cy Young Award did it recently. Who was he?

2. Can you remember Lou Gehrig's replacement at first base?

3. Name the men responsible for ending Joe DiMaggio's 56-day hitting streak.

4. Who caught Aaron's 715th home run in the Braves' bullpen?

5. A National League All-Star appeared as an extra in *The Godfather, Part II*. Who was he?

6. Who played Jimmy Piersall in the film *Fear Strikes Out*?

7. Who drove in the run to snap Don Drysdale's record string of shutout innings?

8. In 1968, Catfish Hunter pitched a perfect game. His final victim was whom?

9. Enos Slaughter made his famous sprint from first base on a single. Who hit the single?

10. Who was the last man to get 200 hits in one year and not bat .300?

11. As of the end of the 1979 season, there were three major-league players who had never played one day in the minor leagues. Name them.

12. What major leaguer played for the Detroit Pistons?

1. Mike Marshall, 1974.
2. Babe Dahlgren.
3. Jim Bagby, Jr.;
   Al Smith; and
   Kenny Keltner.
4. Tom House, a
   Braves pitcher.
5. Steve Garvey.
6. Anthony Perkins.
7. Howie Bedell,
   Philadelphia Phillies.
8. Rich Reese,
   Minnesota Twins.
9. Harry Walker.
10. Matty Alou.
11. Dave Winfield,
    Bob Horner, and
    Catfish Hunter.
12. Ron Reed.

(QUICKIE QUIZ) 2

The Quickie Quiz

1. Who holds the highest one-season pinch-hitting average?

2. Name the man who holds the record for hitting home runs in consecutive games.

3. Ted Williams said this pitcher threw so hard, he couldn't see the ball. Name him.

4. Can you remember the two teams that played in the first televised game?

5. What player was once traded for a manager?

6. A 20-game winner was punched out by Billy Martin. Who was he?

7. Dennis Dummitt, UCLA's fine quarterback of the

late 1960s, was only a backup quarterback in high school. Who was that starter (he became a baseball player)?

8. Can you remember the lowest average ever to win a batting title?

9. Name the catcher who caught more major league games than anyone else.

10. Who was Sandy Koufax's record-setting strikeout victim in the 1963 World Series?

11. The final legal spitball pitcher in the majors was whom?

12. Babe Ruth finished his major league career as a coach. Name the team.

13. Which pitchers stopped Pete Rose's 44-game hitting streak.

ANSWERS:

1. Ed Kranepool, 1974, .486.
2. Dale Long, Pittsburgh, 1956, 8.
3. Steve Dalkowski, Baltimore.
4. Columbia and Fordham Universities.
5. Manny Sanguillen, for Chuck Tanner.
6. Dave Boswell, Minnesota Twins.
7. Bobby Grich.
8. Carl Yastrzemski, .301, 1968.
9. Al Lopez.
10. Harry Bright.
11. Burleigh Grimes.
12. Brooklyn Dodgers, 1938.
13. Larry McWilliams and Gene Garber.

The Quickie Quiz

1. Who did the San Francisco Giants obtain when they traded George Foster to Cincinnati?

2. In 1963 the Chicago White Sox had two pitchers competing for the final spot on their roster. They kept Dave DeBusschere. Who did they cut?

3. Who is the major league leader in career walks given up?

4. Who were the baserunners when Bobby Thomson hit his homer in the 1951 play-off?

5. In 1962 Whitey Ford had his record streak of shutout innings in the World Series stopped at 32. Whose record did he break?

6. Who is the only pitcher to pitch in all seven games of a World Series?

7. Who holds the record for the most RBIs in one game?

8. When Johnny Vander Meer pitched his second straight no-hitter, who was the final out?

9. For what team does Henry Wiggin pitch?

10. Who wrote the song "Van Lingle Mungo"?

11. What relief pitcher recorded two saves and two wins in a single World Series?

12. According to Alex Johnson, what California Angel teammate once threatened him with a gun?

13. Who holds the major league record for the largest cocaine bust?

ANSWERS:

1. Frank Duffy.
2. Denny McLain.
3. Early Wynn.
4. Whitey Lockman and Clint Hartung (pinch-running for Don Mueller).
5. Babe Ruth's.
6. Darold Knowles, 1973.
7. Jim Bottomley, 12.
8. Leo Durocher.
9. New York Mammoths (Mark Harris novels)
10. Dave Frishberg.
11. Larry Sherry, 1959.
12. Chico Ruiz.
13. Orlando Cepeda.

(QUICKIE QUIZ) 4

The Quickie Quiz

1. Name the only pitcher to ever hit *two* grand slams in one game?

2. Who were the last catchers to lead their leagues in triples?

3. A stripper named Morgana used to kiss ball players during games. Who was the only player to kiss her while she worked?

4. What player, in 1972, recorded over 500 at bats yet knocked in only 12 runs?

5. What former Milwaukee Brewer refused to play on Saturdays because of religious reasons.

6. Name the only player ever to chalk up 3,000 hits and 400 home runs.

7. What two NL players were the only men to be MVPs in consecutive years?

8. What batter is the career leader in striking out?

9. During the 1978 season, what player had over 400 at bats and only two walks?

10. How many World Series games did Don Newcombe win?

11. In 1952 a rookie pitcher was 15–2 and led the NL with a 2.43 ERA, yet didn't win Rookie of the Year. Who didn't and who did?

12. In 1979 Keith Hernandez led the NL in both average and RBIs. Who was the last NLer to do so before him?

13. What team did Denny McLain defeat for his 30th win in 1968?

ANSWERS:

1. Tony Cloninger.
2. Carlton Fisk, AL, 1972; Tim McCarver, NL, 1964.
3. Clete Boyer.
4. Enzo Hernandez, San Diego Padres.
5. Danny Thomas.
6. Carl Yastrzemski.
7. Ernie Banks, 1958–59; Joe Morgan, 1975–76.
8. Willie Stargell.
9. Rob Picciolo, Oakland A's.
10. None.
11. Hoyt Wilhelm of the Giants lost to Joe Black of the Dodgers.
12. Tommy Davis in 1962.
13. Oakland.

The Quickie Quiz

1. Who is the career leader in World Series slugging average?

2. Who hit the line drive into Dizzy Dean's big toe?

3. Who hit the line drive into Herb Score's eye?

4. Who was the youngest man to play in a World Series?

5. Who holds the record for most home runs in one month?

6. Who is the only man to play in the Little League World Series and the World Series?

7. Who holds the single-season record for pinch hits?

8. Who did the Mets trade for Joe Foy?

9. Of whom did Casey Stengel say, "He's a fine boy of twenty, and in ten years, he has a chance to be thirty?"

10. Who hit more batters than anyone else in baseball history?

11. Where did the following players play college ball: Sal Bando; Tom Seaver; Dave Winfield; Steve Garvey; Pete Broberg; Ralph Garr; Don Kessinger?

12. Name the only major leaguer ever to appear in a Robert Altman film.

13. Name the pitcher who pitched a no-hitter in his first major league start?

1. Reggie Jackson.
2. Earl Averill.
3. Gil McDougald.
4. Ken Brett.
5. Rudy York (18).
6. Boog Powell.
7. Jose Morales (25, 1976).
8. Amos Otis and Bob Johnson.
9. Greg Goossen.
10. Walter Johnson.
11. Arizona State; USC; Minnesota; Florida; Dartmouth; Grambling; Mississippi State.
12. Jim Bouton, in *The Long Goodbye*.
13. Bobo Holloman.

(QUICKIE QUIZ) 6

The Quickie Quiz

1. Where did Sandy Koufax go to college and what kind of a scholarship did he have?

2. When Dennis Eckersley was traded to the Boston Red Sox in 1978, what did his wife do?

3. Who broke up Tom Seaver's bid for a perfect game in 1969?

4. Who was the only Buddhist outfielder in the majors?

5. Who were the five Yankees to hit over 20 homers in 1961?

6. What is so unusual about the San Diego Padres' manager in 1980?

7. Name the pitcher who yielded Ted William's first major league hit?

8. Who was the on-deck batter when the Giants' Bobby Thomson hit the "shot heard around the world" off Ralph Branca in the 1951 play-off?

9. During the 1946 season, only one regular American League player was not struck out by Bob Feller. Who was he?

10. How many career stolen bases did Babe Ruth have?

11. Who holds the AL record for most games hitting a home run right- and left-handed?

12. In 1927 Babe Ruth began his 60-homer season (154 games) by hitting No. 1 off Howard Ehmke of the Philadelphia A's. Who gave up No. 60?

13. In 1961 Roger Maris hit 61 homers (163 games). He hit the recordbreaking No. 61 off Tracy Stallard of the Red Sox. Off whom did he hit No. one?

ANSWERS:
1. U. of Cincinnati; basketball.
2. She moved in with Indians outfielder Rick Manning.
3. Jim Qualls.
4. Willie Davis.
5. Mickey Mantle, Roger Maris, John Blanchard, Yogi Berra, Elston Howard.
6. Jerry Coleman, former Yankee, had been broadcaster for the Padres for the last eight years.
7. Charles "Red" Ruffing.
8. The Say Hey Kid, Willie Mays.
9. Barney McCoskey, Philadelphia A's.
10. 123.
11. Switch-hitting slugger Mickey Mantle accomplished this feat ten times.

12. Tom Zachary, Washington Senators.
13. Paul Foytack, Detroit Tigers.

The Quickie Quiz

1. Whom did the Red Sox obtain for Sparky Lyle?
2. What brother combo finished one-two in a batting championship?
3. At the age of 20, Al Kaline hit .340 for the 1955 Tigers. What major league record did he set doing this?
4. Who spoiled three no-hitters with a hit in the ninth inning?
5. For which NL team did the Japanese star Masanori Murakami pitch?
6. How many games did the Yankees play from 1931 to 1935 without being shut out?
7. Which team hit the fewest homers in one season?
8. What is the record for most men left on base in a nine-inning contest?
9. Who was the NL's first pinch hitter?
10. How old was Dazzy Vance when he won his first NL game?
11. Who was the first player to win a batting championship without hitting a home run all season?

ANSWERS:

1. Danny Cater.
2. Matty Alou (.342) nosed out brother Felipe Alou (.327) in 1966.
3. Kaline became the youngest ball player to win a batting title.
4. In 1970 Horace Clarke of the Yankees broke up no-hit bids by Joe Niekro, Sonny Siebert, and Jim Rooker.
5. The 1964–65 Giants.
6. 308.
7. The 1908 Chicago White Sox hit three round-trippers.
8. The Yankees left 20 against the Red Sox on September 21, 1956.
9. John "Dirty Jack" Doyle, appearing on June 7, 1892.
10. Vance was 31.
11. Minnesota's Rod Carew, who hit .318 in 1972.

(QUICKIE QUIZ) 8

The Quickie Quiz

1. Who made the only error in the first All-Star game?
2. What do Ernie Banks and O. J. Simpson have in common?
3. The last hit Roberto Clemente ever got was the ——th of his career.

4. What is the only team in big league history to have had three players steal 50 or more bases in one season?

5. What pitcher gave up the most home runs in his career?

6. Before 1980, who was the only Philadelphia Phillies pitcher to win a World Series game?

7. Who is the only pitcher to start an All-Star Game for both leagues?

8. How many grand slams have been hit in All-Star play?

9. Who is the only pitcher to throw a no-hitter in his first game?

10. He has played in more World Series games than anyone else. Who is he?

ANSWERS:
1. Lou Gehrig.
2. Their families: they are second cousins.
3. It was his 3,000th hit. It came on September 30, 1972 off Jon Matlack.
4. The 1976 Oakland A's—Bill North, 75; Bert Campernaris, 54; and Don Baylor, 52.
5. Robin Roberts (502, in 19 seasons).
6. Grover Cleveland Alexander (who was later portrayed in a movie by Ronald Reagan) in game one, 1915. The score was 3–1.
7. Vida Blue in 1971 and 1978.
8. None.
9. On the last day of the 1892 season Charlie Jones earned that distinction pitching for the Cincinnati Reds against the Pittsburgh Pirates. Jones won

only one more game after that, and his lifetime record was an undistinguished 2–4.

10. Yogi Berra. In 14 Fall Classics Berra played in 75 games. With free agency and expansion it is unlikely that this record will ever be broken.

The Quickie Quiz

1. What is the oldest park in the major leagues?

2. What city has been the home of a last-place club most times?

3. How many sluggers have 3,000 hits but lifetime averages under .300?

4. Who was the best hitting pitcher (over 500 at bats)?

5. What was the most lopsided win in World Series history?

6. What were the most runs scored in one inning before and after 1900?

7. Who wrote "Take Me Out to the Ballgame"?

8. The largest crowd in baseball history was at what stadium and when?

9. Who was the oldest player ever to play in the major leagues?

10. What was the first major league?

11. How many black umpires have there been in the major leagues?

ANSWERS:

1. Comiskey Park, Chicago (1910).
2. Philadelphia (42).
3. Carl Yastrzemski, Lou Brock, and Al Kaline.
4. George Uhle (Detroit) (.288 career average).
5. 1960 (N.Y. Yankees 16, Pittsburgh 0).
6. Chicago Cubs, seventh inning, Sept. 6, 1883 (18).
   Boston (AL), seventh inning, June 18, 1953 (17).
7. Words by Jack Norworth, music by Albert von Tilzer.
8. 84,587 at Cleveland on Sept. 12, 1954 (regular season).
   92,706 at L.A. Coliseum on Oct. 6, 1959 (World Series).
9. Satchel Paige started his career at the age of 42 and ended it at 59.
10. National Association of Professional Baseball Players, 1871.
11. Three (Emmet Ashford, Art Williams and Eric Gregg).

GREAT TRIVIA BOOKS
FROM WARNER BOOKS

THE COMPLETE UNABRIDGED SUPER TRIVIA ENCYCLOPEDIA
by Fred L. Worth   (V96-905, $3.50)
Xavier Cugat's theme song? The bestseller of 1929? Miss Hungary of 1936? Here's more than 800 pages of pure entertainment for collectors, gamblers, crossword puzzle addicts and those who want to stroll down memory lane. It asks every question, answers it correctly, solves every argument.

HOLLYWOOD TRIVIA
by David P. Strauss & Fred L. Worth   (V95-492, $2.75)
Spotlighting the characters that made Hollywood happen, here are thousands of film facts that will delight and surprise you. Who was buried wearing vampire gear? Who stood on a box to appear taller than his leading lady? Why couldn't Clark Gable secure the leading role in *Little Caesar*? Almost 400 pages of fact and history.

CELEBRITY TRIVIA
by Edward Lucaire   (V95-479, $2.75)
Crammed with gossip galore, this book was written with the name-dropper in all of us in mind. It's loaded with public and private memorabilia on actors, writers, rock stars, tyrants—and the scandalous facts they probably wouldn't want you to know. From Napoleon to Alice Cooper, anyone who has caught the public eye is fair game.

THIRTY YEARS OF ROCK 'N' ROLL TRIVIA
by Fred L. Worth   (V91-494, $2.50)
Who thought up the name Chubby Checker? Who was paid $10,000 *not* to appear on the Ed Sullivan Show? Who made his television debut with his fly open? A fascinating and colorful compendium of pop memorabilia for both the casual fan and serious afficianado.

THE BEST OF BESTSELLERS
FROM WARNER BOOKS

THE NEXT
by Bob Randall   **(95-740, $2.75)**

A growing boy! That's what Kate's ten-year-old nephew was. Yet during the weeks he was left in her care—while his mother recovered from a car accident—Charles was growing at an astonishing rate. Love can turn a boy into a man. But evil can do it faster.

THE FAN
by Bob Randall   **(95-887, $2.75)**

The Fan: warm and admiring, then arrogantly suggestive; then obscene, and finally, menacing. Plunging a dawdy Broadway actress into a shocking nightmare. "A real nail-biter . . . works to perfection as it builds to a surprising climax . . . the tension is killing."
                                                  —*Saturday Review*

FORT APACHE, THE BRONX
by Heywood Gould   **(95-618, $2.75)**

They were only rookies . . . two green cops blown away on the killer walkways of the Bronx. Now the Force is on the prowl under a tough new captain who is determined to shape up his last command for losers where life is mean, death is often murder, and the law of the jungle is the only law.

SEE THE KID RUN
by Bob Ottum   **(91-123, $2.50)**

A chilling race through the dark side of New York with a kid you'll never forget! Wanted: Elvis Presley Reynolds, aged 14½, who dreams of Mark Cross, Brooks Brothers and the Plaza—where one day soon he'll pass as "Somebody." He's an urban urchin with bottomless eyes and an incredible ambition to escape to the good life while there's still time.

THE TUESDAY BLADE
by Bob Ottum   **(91-643, $2.50)**

"We're looking for one guy carrying seven razors or seven guys carrying one razor each." That's how a cop summed up the case. But the killer they were tracking was just one girl—big, beautiful and armed with THE TUESDAY BLADE. "My current reading favorite . . . makes 'Death Wish' look like a kindergarten exercise."
                                                  —Liz Smith, *New York News*